BLEND
collection ◀

GENESIS
MANNEQUINS

www.genesis-display.com

It began with a spark... it has burned for 333 years.

The difference is **Gaggenau.**

In 1683, from the depths of the Black Forest, a flame sprang to life and the age of the industrial craftsmanship began. From the same process that saw a forge emerge, the invention of the Badenia bicycle and the introduction of the combi-steam oven to the private kitchen, we have always imagined what could be. Then built it.

333 years of working with metal is an achievement only few can claim. It exposes a success that has crossed time, distance and cultures. Gaggenau is not just a kitchen appliance; it is the soul of a home and it is this passion that has been 333 years in the making.

For more information, please visit www.gaggenau.com.

EXPLORE THE FIGURA COLLECTION

FIGURA COLLECTION

Push your floor design in a completely new direction. With the Figura collection, you have shape, material and colour entirely in your hands to tailor your floor into a truly unique experience. Combining the flexibility and environmental values of carpet tiles with creative and playful shapes in different materials and colours, Figura delivers head-turning designs that match any room and requirement. Explore space by going bold with powerful contrasts or create a subtle, refined ambience by using different materials in the same colour tone. **Learn more at egecarpets.com**

THE URGE TO EXPLORE SPACE

CONTENTS

Photo Danica O. Kus

On page 092, Olafur Eliasson's retrospective leads visitors through a labyrinth of colour.

017
Seeds FRAM3

We go from atelier to laboratory in search of what's bubbling on the fringes of the great indoors

039
Portraits

040
Patricia Urquiola
'I'm not a visionary'

045
Ronald Hooft
Tongue-in-cheek trendcasting

046
John Sabraw FRAM3
Doing the dirty work

050
Studio Makkink & Bey FRAM3
Two lives, one story

052
Freitag FRAM3
The F-abric journey

057
Partisans FRAM3
Taking on Toronto

062
Humanscale FRAM3
Todd Bracher's wearable chair

066
The Collector FRAM3
At home with the Stones

070
Ciguë
Driven by intuition

076
Ege
Getting flexible with Figura

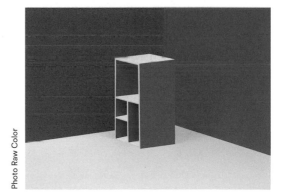

Photo Raw Color

Lex Pott turns the tables on page 025.

Photo Antonio Campanella

Patricia Urquiola uncloaks her creative tale on page 040.

081
Harvest

The pick of the crop: a visual feast plucked from the worlds of art and design

Photo Nicholas Calcott

Jordana Maisie's interior for Feit stacks up on page 116.

Features

130
Deyan Sudjic [FRAME]
Playing the long game

139
Frame Lab [FRAME]
Work It Out
140
How physical space affects creativity
144
Studio O+A's human-centric workspaces
150
Five steps to future-proof offices

Photo Mate Moro

Turn to page 130 to hear Deyan Sudjic of London's Design Museum talk shop.

— FRAME LAB —
WORK
Catering to today's commercial crowd
139

Articles featuring this logo allow you to view extra content in the digital magazine

Check out page 181 to see how Freund's Moss Walls give a green dimension to interiors.

177
IMM Trends
Sense and sensibility in flooring, wallcoverings and sanitary

193
The Great Indoors Award
Show-stealing interiors

202
Febrik
Making waves with Drop

204
Short Cut
Chubby suds sculptures

206
The Reissue
Born again: Joe Colombo's Square System

208
In Numbers [FRAME]
Alec Momont's Ambulance Drone in facts and figures

BETTELUX SHAPE

The new design concept in an open steel frame.
Made from high-grade steel/enamel with a 30 year warranty.

Design: Tesseraux + Partner

BETTE

Frame is published six times a year by

Frame Publishers
Laan der Hesperiden 68
NL-1076 DX Amsterdam
T +31 20 423 3717
F +31 20 428 0653
frame@frameweb.com
frameweb.com

Editorial

EDITOR IN CHIEF
Robert Thiemann – **RT**

MANAGING EDITOR
Tracey Ingram – **TI**

EDITORS
Floor Kuitert – **FK**
Maria Elena Oberti – **MO**

EDITORIAL INTERN
Christian Walters – **CW**

COPY EDITORS
InOtherWords (D'Laine Camp,
Donna de Vries-Hermansader)

DESIGN DIRECTOR
Barbara Iwanicka

GRAPHIC DESIGNERS
Vincent Hammingh
Cathelijn Kruunenberg

TRANSLATION
InOtherWords (Maria van Tol,
Donna de Vries-Hermansader)

**CONTRIBUTORS
TO THIS ISSUE**
Nicola Bozzi – **NB**
Giovanna Dunmall – **GD**

Will Georgi – **WG**
Lilia Glanzmann – **LG**
Daniel Golling – **DG**
Kanae Hasegawa – **KH**
Ronald Hooft – **RH**
Adrian Madlener – **AM**
Lara Mikocki – **LM**
Enya Moore – **EM**
Shonquis Moreno – **SM**
Jonathan Openshaw – **JO**
Elizabeth Pagliacolo – **EP**
Jeannette Petrik – **JP**
Jane Szita – **JS**
Anne van der Zwaag – **AvdZ**

WEB EDITOR
Lauren Grieco
lauren@frameweb.com

COVER
Image Akatre

LITHOGRAPHY
Edward de Nijs

PRINTING
Grafisch Bedrijf Tuijtel
Hardinxveld-Giessendam

Publishing

DIRECTORS
Robert Thiemann
Rudolf van Wezel

**SALES AND MARKETING
DIRECTOR**
Margreet Nanning
margreet@frameweb.com

BRAND MANAGER
Hanneke Stuij
hanneke@frameweb.com

**DISTRIBUTION
AND LOGISTICS**
Nick van Oppenraaij
nick@frameweb.com

FINANCE
Cedric Isselt
cedric@frameweb.com

Pearl Yssel
pearl@frameweb.com

Advertising

SALES MANAGERS
Nikki Brandenburg
nikki@frameweb.com

Sarah Maisey
sarahmaisey@frameweb.com

**ADVERTISING
REPRESENTATIVES**

Italy
Studio Mitos
Michele Tosato
T +39 0422 894 868
michele@studiomitos.it

Turkey
Titajans
Hilmi Zafer Erdem
T +90 212 257 76 66
titajans@titajans.com
Licence holders

LICENCE HOLDERS

Korea
Tong Yang Media Co. Ltd.
Young Lee
T +82 70 8169 6013
framekorea@gmail.com

QUERIES
service@frameweb.com

BOOKSTORE DISTRIBUTORS
Frame is available at sales
points worldwide.
Please see frameweb.com/
magazines/where-to-buy.

Frame (USPS No: 019-372) is
published bimonthly by Frame
Publishers NL and distributed
in the USA by Asendia USA, 17B
South Middlesex Ave., Monroe,
NJ 08831. Periodicals postage
paid at New Brunswick, NJ, and
additional mailing offices.

Postmaster: send address
changes to *Frame*, 701C
Ashland Ave., Folcroft,
PA 19032.

ISSN FRAME: 1388-4239

Subscribe

Regular subscription
From €99
Introductory 1-year subscription
From €79
Student subscription
From €69

Visit frameweb.com/subscribe
for more options or e-mail us at
service@frameweb.com.

Back issues
Buy online at store.frameweb.com

Frame 107   *Frame* 106   *Frame* 105   *Frame* 104

feel the difference

Our philosophy is to challenge what has become habitual, and to never be satisfied with anything less than the best. We seek perfection each and every day and ensure that our leather meets all international quality requirements and technical specifications. We contribute to long-term and sustainable development while continuously reducing the impact on the environment. Through our Custom-colour-program we can now offer more than 10,000 colours for you to enjoy. They are all skin deep and full of emotions. You will feel the difference!

leather by elmo★

No More Nine to Five

Chances are that you see this magazine as professional literature. You draw inspiration from its pages and catch up on the latest developments with an eye to raising the level of your own work. But I doubt that you read *Frame* at the office. The office is mainly a place for meetings and brainstorming sessions. A lot of your 'work' gets done at home or on the way – maybe in an airport lounge, where you're not the only one who flips open a laptop. Occasionally when that happens, you might wonder whether a physical office is something we still need. And, if we do, what are its requirements now that we carry our office in a handy bag that allows us to work anytime, anywhere?

Imagine travelling back in time, say a century ago, when most people worked at home or not far from home. In those days, there was little distinction between where you lived and where you worked. The big difference is the number of people who worked for themselves in the early 20th century instead of belonging to an organization, which is the norm today. It's precisely that change that gave birth to the office as we know it: a physical space that represents an organization and provides staff with a professional home base.

So what does the ideal office look like? Because it functions chiefly as a showpiece, it gives outsiders a clear idea of what the organization stands for, while reminding employees of the principles they are meant to share. The contemporary office helps people to be as productive as possible in an environment that not only fosters concentration but also has facilities for group discussions. Needed are chill-out areas combined with opportunities to move and exercise. Sitting is all right, but not for too long, because recent reports on health hazards compare sitting to smoking. Daylight is a must, as long as it's not too bright or distracting, and so is an abundance of plants, which purify the air. And finally, today's office may not emphasize hierarchy in any way. People perform best when they feel free, safe and connected – and not when they are hampered by pressure or seclusion.

Sounds easy, doesn't it? A more in-depth analysis of the subject begins on page 139, in a section that lists all the ingredients for a successful office design.

It might be nice to ingest that information along with a latte macchiato in the 'library', 'shelter' or 'town hall' of your modern office. Or while waiting for your next flight, of course.

Robert Thiemann, Editor in Chief
robert@frameweb.com

X-Code

Design: Daniel Figueroa

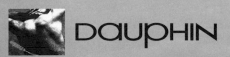

daUPHIN

Illustrations Andrea Wan

'Norah and Norman Stone integrate design and art into every aspect of their life. Their collection - the result of a personal approach to artists and designers - beautifully displays their personalities'

Anne van der Zwaag is a Dutch cultural entrepreneur with an interest in creative crossovers: she writes about art, photography, fashion, design and architecture. Van der Zwaag works as a curator at home and abroad. She is the director of design fair Object Rotterdam and a passionate collector of design and art. In this edition of *Frame*, she interviews fellow design enthusiasts Norman and Norah Stone, who discuss the ins and outs of collecting.

'It was a treat to capture Deyan Sudjic: he has a dynamic character and so much energy. The Design Museum was a nice minimalist backdrop for the shoot, which perfectly suited his personality'

Hungary's **Mate Moro** is a London-based photographer and art director specializing in fashion and advertising. Since graduating with a Master of Arts degree from Moholy-Nagy University of Art and Design in Budapest, Moro has worked for various brands – L.K.Bennett, Bionda Castana, Baraboux, Use Unused – and for magazines like *Tank* and *The Room*. His portrait of Deyan Sudjic, director of the Design Museum in London, appears in *Frame* 108.

'I've known Alexander since we were kids, so it was really exciting to have an opportunity to work with him and Partisans as adults. I'm so impressed by what they are doing and by the atmosphere of their office. It's a really inspiring place'

After graduating from Ryerson University in 2006 with a degree in fashion design, Toronto's **Caitlin Cronenberg** went on to pursue a career in photography. Her work has been featured in *L'Uomo Vogue*, *Elle* (French edition), *Pulp*, *Vanity Fair* (German edition), *25 Magazine*, *Hello! Canada* and *Filler*, among others. In 2010 she self-published *Poser*, her first book of photography; she is currently working on a second volume: *The Endings*. For *Frame* 108, Cronenberg shot local architecture and design firm Partisans.

'When we started the project, we had no idea how valuable creativity was for the modern worker. It was exciting and a privilege to speak to some of the world's biggest thinkers in workplace design as part of our research'

Oliver Marlow is a pioneer of the co-working movement and an expert on the relationship between space, collaboration and creativity. In 2013 he coauthored *Codesigning Space* and he's now working on another book, *Spaces for Innovation*, with **Kursty Groves Knight**. As adjunct professor at the IE University in Madrid, she leads a master's course in Agile Work Space Design. Marlow and Groves Knight share insights into the future of the workplace in this issue's Frame Lab.

'The experience of photographing John Sabraw and being in his studio gave me a window into the mind of an artistic genius. The transformation seen in his canvases is fascinating, and his quirks put a smile on my face for days'

Artist and lifestyle photographer **Louise O'Rourke** lives and works in Philadelphia. The holder of an MFA in photography from Ohio University, she shares her knowledge at the Philadelphia Photo Arts Center, where she teaches. In June 2015 she opened non-profit organization Kitchen Table Gallery. *Frame* called on O'Rourke to capture artist John Sabraw at work.

'I expected the studio to look like the shops Ciguë designs: clean and minimalist. I was surprised to be welcomed by a big prolific mess. The location was as inspiring as the people it housed'

Originally from the south of France, fashion and editorial photographer **Fiona Torre** works and lives in Paris. Torre's clientele includes publications such as *Le Monde*, *Jalouse* and *Vanity Fair*, as well as brands like American Apparel, Christian Lacroix and Vitra. For this issue of *Frame*, she visited the Montreuil studio of architecture collective Ciguë.

proportion >london

THEORY

www.proportionlondon.com

Seeds

Designers see the wood for the trees. Super-natural shines at Cersaie. Boeing introduces the world's lightest material. Fashion brands serve up feasts. Concrete shapes an unconventional spa experience. All this and more is bubbling on the fringes of the great indoors.

Concrete Comfort

Matter Design
questions the
notion of comfort
through an
unconventional
spa experience

Standing in a confined space surrounded by nothing but concrete is more reminiscent of a prison cell than a spa. Nevertheless, Matter Design's radiant bath installation, Microtherme, offered the experience to those who attended Bigger than a Breadbox, Smaller than a Building, a BSA-curated exhibition in Boston, Massachusetts.

Entering the room that showcased Microtherme, visitors were confronted with a hovering birch-plywood structure containing – and shielding from view – the entirety of the futuristic bath. Childish curiosity led many to slide beneath the box and find themselves surrounded by concrete. Small openings within the dense interior environment permitted them to stand and be encased in a thermal and sensorial delight that was somewhat comparable to the feeling you might have while wading in a pool of voluptuous concrete.

The designers used a trio of materials: expanded polystyrene, glass-fibre-reinforced concrete and copper tubing, the last of which allowed water to pass through the concrete and provided a means of temperature control. In its approach to comfort, Microtherme steers clear of the norm and breaks several conventions, yet the lulling warmth and wash of calm override the object's bizarre character. Cement, a vital ingredient of concrete, has found its way into therapeutic treatments, so it's reasonable to believe that Microtherme will not only perplex users but also leave them relaxed and refreshed. — CW
matterdesignstudio.com

A new perspective on tiles

Design by Edward Barber & Jay Osgerby,
Ronan & Erwan Bouroullec, Rodolfo Dordoni,
Konstantin Grcic, Raw Edges, Inga Sempé,
Patricia Urquiola, Tokujin Yoshioka.

mutina.it

terzani.com

Doodle, Freehand *Design*
design Simone Micheli

Up in Smoke

An online shop featuring luxury smoking accessories restores the sex appeal of the cigarette

If you thought smoking had gone out of fashion, well, *puff* again. American journalists Monica Khemsurov, Eviana Hartman, and Su Wu have resurrected the design and supply of high-end cigarette accessories with the launch of their online shop, Tetra. Smoker or not, you'll have to admit that the items on offer are as tasteful as they are tempting. Ashtrays laced with 24-carat gold, finely crafted pipes and ornamental lighters are just a lick's worth of what Tetra offers.

In their *raison d'être*, the brand's founders say they intend to 'elevate the aesthetics of the smoking experience' with products that recall romantic images of mid-20th-century design celebrities such as Dieter Rams, Marianne Brandt and Enzo Mari. A brand established in the face of taboo, Tetra openly celebrates the tradition and allure of the smoking ritual. But don't worry – you can still kick the habit in style; the shop also sells spiffy vaporizers. — LM

shop-tetra.com

2

Kith

Photo Nolan Persons

Fashion brands are hungry for more

Tastemakers

1

Prada

Photo courtesy of Prada

As ultra-skinny mannequins continue to dominate the runways, food might not be the first thing we associate with high fashion. This season, however, clothing brands are debunking clichés and serving up some fashionable feasts.

Milan is the most obvious setting for a combination of fashion and food – two industries rooted in Italian culture. Prada ① cherishes the city's heritage by acquiring 80 per cent of iconic pastry shop Pasticceria Marchesi, an establishment dating back to 1824. Now a welcome addition to Milan's upscale Via Montenapoleone, the new location boasts an interior designed by architect Roberto Baciocchi.

Snarkitecture ② revamps the Brooklyn location of multi-brand store Kith, now enhanced by a slightly unusual feature. In the space between footwear and apparel, shoppers find a cereal bar with an array of goodies sure to fulfil every child's breakfast dreams. Kith Treats offers 23 types of cereal and an equally extensive assortment of milks and toppings.

In London, a space at the Institute of Contemporary Arts turns into a temporary sandwich factory for Molly Goddard's ③ S/S 2016 presentation. In scenes reminiscent of typical teenage summer jobs, models dressed in pastel party-wear take their places along a production line – a clinical-looking decor designed by Sarah Edwards. Safe to say that food ventures like these are the cherry on top of a fashionista's shopping spree. — FK

prada.com
snarkitecture.com
mollygoddard.com

3
Molly Goddard

FRAM3 The digital magazine offers a visual taste of Molly Goddard's treats

Rotating Lex Pott's
Chroma collection
creates a whole
new colour scheme

Building a reputation for his original use of materials, Lex Pott launched another cunningly clever product at Dutch Design Week in October. Pott singled out edge banding – an element of contemporary furniture that's commonly used to mask lower-quality materials – and transformed it into the point of departure for his Chroma collection. By using different colours of edge banding on different faces of the products, Pott developed pieces that look new from every angle. The inclusion of reflective metal laminates in the material palette (Pott selected existing items from Abet Laminati and Homapal) allows certain tones to bounce off others, forming layers of colour. The collection – which was commissioned by Baars & Bloemhoff – may not be customizable in the strictest sense, but Pott caters to the trend by letting individuals pick their palette with a literal turn of the tables. — TI

lexpott.nl

Photo Raw Color

Into the Woods

The world's forests are disappearing at an alarming rate. An industrialized timber industry has made trees into commodities, with no regard for their role as living organisms. Today's environmentally aware artists and designers are reconsidering this traditional material resource. Refusing to waste, they utilize each precious tree from crown to roots. Their goal is a forest that not only regains its ecological value but also recaptures its mysterious, majestic identity. —FK

Photo Simon Armstrong

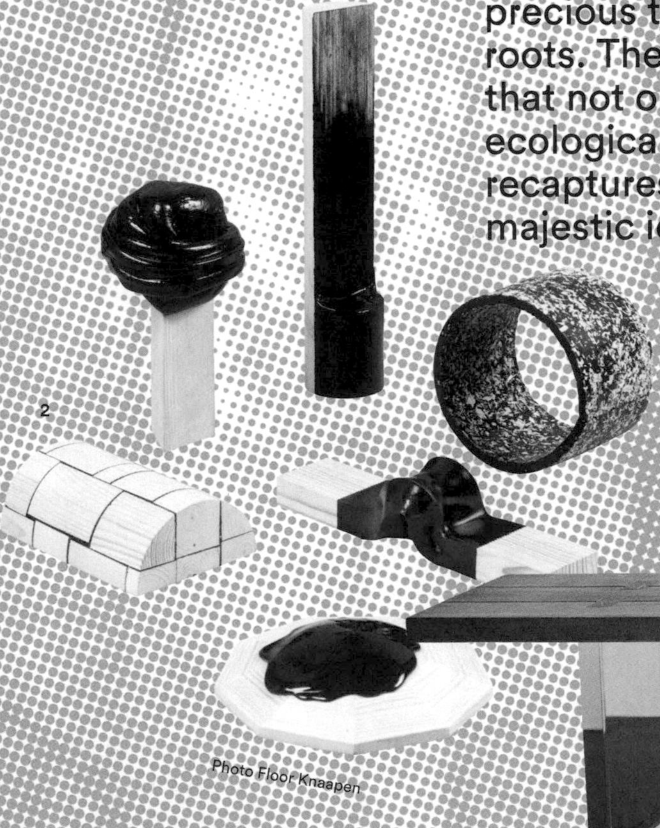

Photo Floor Knaapen

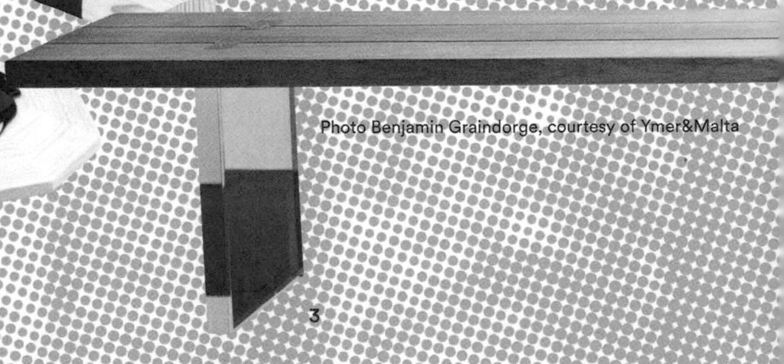

Photo Benjamin Graindorge, courtesy of Ymer&Malta

① For his S/S 2016 collection, James Kelly imagines a woman 'waking up after an event that left her abandoned in a forest'.

② With the support of Creative Industries Fund NL, Studio Thomas Vailly reappraises the resinous *Pinus pinaster* in a research project entitled Reconfiguration of a Tree.

③ Part of Ymer&Malta's Morning Mist collection, Benjamin Graindorge's Fallen Tree bench relies on the branches of an oak tree for its sculptured look.

FRAM3 The digital magazine presents a captivating teaser for In the Eyes of the Animal

5

Photo Luca Marziale, courtesy of Marshmallow Laser Feast

4

Photo Tõnu Tunnel

6

Photo Francisco Nocito

④ Ruup, an acoustic installation that amplifies the sounds of the forest, features supersize wooden megaphones; it is the work of students attending the Estonian Academy of the Arts.

⑤ By means of virtual reality, creative collective Marshmallow Laser Feast lets visitors to its project – In the Eyes of the Animal – experience the forest from the perspective of its inhabitants.

⑥ Textured *ton sur ton* rugs by Argentinian artist Alexandra Kehayoglou are reminiscent of a mossy forest floor.

⑦ Questioning the truth behind claims for so-called green cosmetics, Kingston University graduate Mary Graham introduces truly natural eyelashes.

Refusing to waste, designers utilize each precious tree from crown to roots

Photo Steve Hall, courtesy of Hedrich Blessing

Photo Iris van der Velde

Photo Lisa Klappe

Photo Kristof Vrancken

⑧   A project suitable for mass production, S House is the work of Vo Trong Nghia Architects, which 'aims to provide affordable, durable, and easy-to-construct houses for low-income tropical regions'.

⑨   Betula, a materials research project by Cynthia Oegema, investigates the potential of birch tree products that are generally considered to be unusable.

⑩   Using biomimicry and 3D printing, Lilian van Daal – winner of the Volvo Design Challenge 2015 – crafts a recyclable car seat out of Swedish pine.

⑪   Holder of a master's degree in Social Design from DAE, Sarmite Polakova explores the leathery properties of the pine tree, abundant in her native land of Latvia.

13–18. 3. 2016

Frankfurt am Main

light+building

The world's leading trade fair for
lighting and building services technology

Discover trends.
Shape the future.

Creative lighting designs and smart building systems
technology: Discover how everything is integrated
with everything else and how the trends of tomorrow
are being created. Only at Light + Building, the hotspot
for inspirations and innovations.
Where modern spaces come to life.

www.light-building.com

messe frankfurt

In the digital magazine, Sophia Yang of HRL Laboratories breaks down the 'world's lightest material'

Air in the Air

What Boeing describes as the world's lightest material may allow aircraft design to reach new heights

The next generation of aeroplanes and cars may use a material that's reportedly 100 times lighter than Styrofoam and that has the potential to catapult the automotive industry to new eco-friendly heights. The minds behind this development are from Malibu-based HRL Laboratories, a company (co-owned by Boeing) that has been conducting pioneering research for over 60 years.

The team's 'microlattice' weighs less than the proverbial feather; 99.99 per cent of its composition is air, while the remainder is a series of interconnected hollow metal tubes. Similar to the honeycomb structure of bone, HRL's microlattice is low in density and compressible, a property vital to the absorption of high levels of energy. To begin with, microlattice could be used as structural reinforcement in the realization of lighter, more fuel-efficient aircraft. And the possibilities don't end there. Several other applications have been suggested, such as sound and shock absorption and thermal insulation. Proof that something so small can pack a mighty punch. — **CW**

hrl.com

Photo Dan Little, courtesy of HRL Laboratories LLC

ambiente
the show

12 – 16. 2. 2016

Design that is changing the market. Ideas that develop in discussions. Projects that have their beginnings here. The world's most important consumer goods trade fair sets the future in motion. See for yourself where the market is going. And make sure you're there when visions become opportunities. What a show!

The Design. The Market. The Blog.
ambiente-blog.com

messe frankfurt

Eager to attend the annual Cersaie trade show, flocks of international ceramics enthusiasts poured into Bologna's Fiera district for a taste of the tile industry's finest fare. This year, no fewer than 101,000 visitors turned up, the most the event has ever attracted. Setting the scene were *super*-natural imitations, textural nuances and cross-disciplinary fusions. — MO

Tiles for Miles

5

2

4

1

3

6

① Ceramica Sant'Agostino's Blendart collection merges the rustic aesthetics of authentic wood flooring with the DNA of porcelain tile. Blendart's virtually unlimited colour and grain variations rely on the latest in digital ink-jet printing.

② Inspired by architectural drawings done by hand, Lea Ceramische's Naïve range, designed by Patrick Norguet, is distinguished by a seemingly random network of intersecting lines. Part of the Slimtech Series, the tiles come in a spectrum of soft hues.

③ Taking its cue from the natural world, Casalgrande Padana's Pietre di Paragone porcelain tiles recall the raw aesthetics of granite and limestone. The collection is available in six sizes and three textures.

④ An illusion of abstract three-dimensional volumes generated by a play of light and shadow defines Tagina's DeTails. Choose from glazed or matte finishes in any of nine colours.

⑤ Designed by Nendo, Brix's Micro-Brick collection alludes to traditional building methods. Available in seven patterns, the miniature tiles, each only 5 x 10 mm, simulate the look of classic masonry.

⑥ Five delicate patterns in relief – Diamante, Line, Curve, Square and Rose – highlight Lumina, a series of all-white ceramic tiles from Fap.

⑦ With slabs as large as 120 x 140 cm, Ceramiche Caesar's Project Evolution series

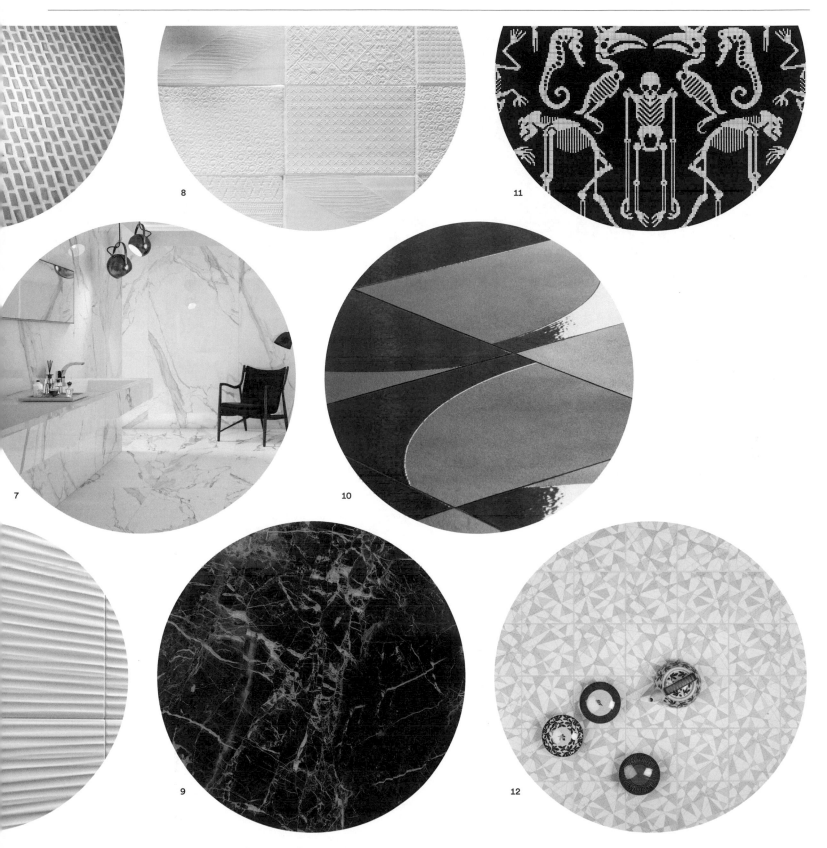

7

8

9

10

11

12

diminishes the intrusion of grout lines to produce a seamless stone-like finish.

⑧ Signs, a collection of tiles from 41zero42, comprises a mix of six imprinted, artisanal tiles. The porcelain pieces, which are not sold separately, can be combined to create an intricate patchwork of textures and patterns.

⑨ For its Allmarble ceramic collection, Marazzi employs state-of-the-art production technology to mimic genuine marble. In addition to three standard finishes – lux, natural and structured – choices now include ultra-smooth silk.

⑩ For his first collaboration with Mutina, Konstantin Grcic whipped up Numi, a minimalist range of glazed and matte ceramic tiles. The German designer's subtle fusion and inversion of finishes provide the basis for an endless array of geometric compositions.

⑪ Sparked by an interest in archaeological discoveries and the 'historical arts', Studio Job developed Perished for Bisazza. The Belgian designers' contemporary take on the neogothic comes in two colourways: black and white or rose-gold and brown.

⑫ Living Ceramics teamed up with Spain's José Manuel Ferrero to give rise to Warp, a new addition to the company's Signature Surfaces series. A nod to London's Savile Row – aka the golden mile of made-to-measure menswear – the 15-x-15-cm tiles make reference to bespoke tailoring.

Photos courtesy of Adidas

Custom Kicks

Adidas and Materialise
develop a 3D-printed
prototype set to send
runners sprinting into
the future

As any athlete knows, having the proper performance gear goes a long way. In collaboration with 3D-printing experts at Belgian outfit Materialise, sportswear brand Adidas gives us a glimpse of Futurecraft 3D, which it considers the ultimate in athletic footwear. Prototypes of the trainer, being developed to offer users high-tech speed and comfort based on innovative manufacturing and design, are 'in testing and limited production' as we speak. One experiment involves a treadmill that measures the unique pressure points and contours of an individual's feet while running. Using the latest in foot-scan and 3D-printing technology, the team focuses on the midsole, the shock-absorbing layer between the shoe's inner and outer soles. The midsole is laser-sintered in TPU (thermoplastic polyurethane). The forerunner to a potential line of Adidas shoes, the concept introduces a modern approach to existing made-to-measure products. — **LM**

a d i d a s . c o m
m a t e r i a l i s e . c o m

 Check out the Futurecraft 3D
film in the digital magazine

SQUARESPACE

Build it beautiful

WEBSITES • DOMAINS • COMMERCE + MORE

Build a beautiful website with Squarespace.
Start your free trial today. No credit card required.

USE THE OFFER CODE "FRAME" TO SAVE 10%.

Stay <u>On Top</u> With Us <u>Stockholm</u> Furniture & Light Fair February <u>9–13</u> 2016

stockholmfurniturefair.com
northernlightfair.com
stockholmdesignweek.com

It's a fact – when we interact with people with similar minds and dreams they become valuable not only to our senses but to our business. Be one of the first to capture the essence of new trends at the world's largest meeting place for Scandinavian design. Just outside the beautiful city of Stockholm over 700 unique design companies have made it possible for you to see their work. Be inspired, by the most exciting lecturers among the established and the up and coming within the business at the Stockholm Design Talks. Or get your kick out of the unique inspirational exhibitions. It's a perfect venue for creating opportunities to establish new and inspiring contacts, which will be beneficial to both parties. Stay on top – visit a fair with a Scandinavian flair.

While here – Stockholm Design Week is also up and running in the city during the same week as the Stockholm Furniture & Light Fair.

Stockholm Furniture Fair®
Stockholm Design Week®
Northern Light Fair™

Stockholmsmässan

Telling Tales

Daniela Treija sees new design possibilities in works of fiction

With ivy-green binding and the words *Form Follows Fiction* imprinted on its surface, Daniela Treija's tactile volume could easily be mistaken for a novel. But Treija didn't spend her final year at Design Academy Eindhoven writing a book. For her slick 'encyclopaedia of the imaginary', Treija read novels and watched movies, plucking out fantastical objects that she could 'revive'. It's not unheard of for speculative items from the realm of fiction to end up as actual products – think Nike's self-lacing shoes from *Back to the Future Part II* – but Treija believes her method offers a recipe for 'envisioning new possibilities' in the field of design. The book reveals 83 sketches that include everything from Mary Poppins' bottomless bag to a breadknife – like the one in *The Hitchhiker's Guide to the Galaxy* – that cuts and toasts simultaneously. So far, Treija has turned three of her designs into physical objects; the remaining 80 act as a 'guide to design speculation'. — EM

danielatreija.com

Portraits

Partisans aims high in Toronto. Patricia Urquiola reflects on where it all began. John Sabraw paints with pollution. Norman and Norah Stone open the doors to their collection. Ciguë traces its aesthetic roots. Rianne Makkink and Jurgen Bey offer a window into their world. All this and more perspectives on people.

'Women are very flexible, very
open to change,' says Patricia
Urquiola. 'We practise being
adaptable in our jobs as well.'

Born in Spain but based in Italy, Patricia Urquiola believes empathy rather than style defines her as a designer.

WORDS *Floor Kuitert* PORTRAITS *Antonio Campanella*

ADOPT, ADAPT, ACT

'I GREW up with a mother who was not always cooking, like many other Italian mammas. She didn't like cooking at all. But in the summer and on weekends we often went to my grandfather's beach house, a half-hour's drive from my birthplace, Oviedo, in the coastal town of Salinas. [Urquiola designed the Salinas kitchen for Boffi.] The house had a big messy kitchen with a table in the middle – not for eating but for working. Whenever you got anywhere near that table, someone would ask for your help. You'd end up cutting bread or cleaning fish. It's the first laboratory I can remember.'

'When I became a designer, my mother said: "How is it possible? You were always breaking down the house!" I was a very curious child, constantly trying to understand things by opening them and taking them apart. She's right – I did break down the house. In the end, there was always a piece left that didn't seem to fit anywhere. Typically a child who's cut out to be a designer, I think.'

'At school, there was a very old workshop where we learned to make things with our hands. I had a very intellectual friend, who now writes for the theatre – she really hated that class, just like another friend who I believe became a lawyer. I used to do all their work. I loved it.'

'When you think of people that work with their hands, it doesn't mean the instrument of thinking is not there. The two are well connected.'

'My mother went to London a lot. I remember her coming back with a necklace made of hair, which she'd seen in a presentation. She also bought fake lashes from Mary Quant. I was ten or 11 when she took me and my cousin with her. We didn't travel very much back then. We went to Liberty, the department store. It was dark inside, with this 1920s atmosphere – fantastic. There was a restaurant on the top floor that was like a rainbow and fitting rooms where you were all together. It's so different now.'

'My mom studied philosophy. She was not the typical mom – our circumstances were different – but she was a fantastic lady. We got a lot of advice from our parents, who encouraged my three brothers to leave home. "Spain is little. Move! Learn languages, get out of your comfort zone," they would say. I believe in that as well. It makes for a quicker evolution of your personality. It gives you confidence.'

'At a young age I knew I wanted to study architecture. My grandmother's brother was an architect, and two cousins on my mother's side were with architects. It interested me. My ⤷

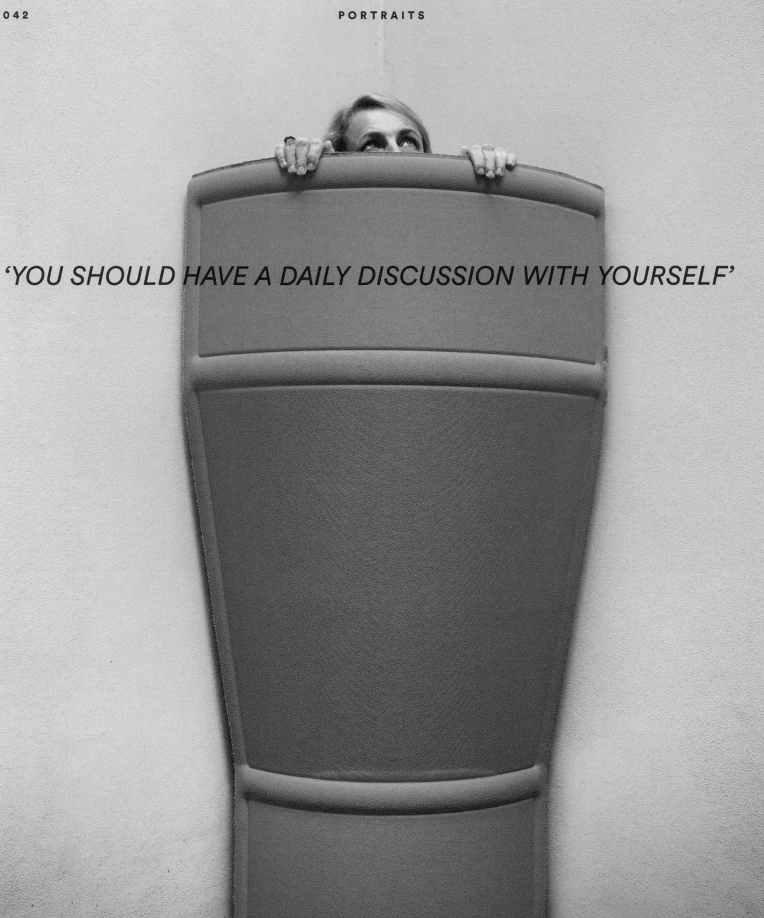

'YOU SHOULD HAVE A DAILY DISCUSSION WITH YOURSELF'

Urquiola believes it's important to get out of your comfort zone, as 'it makes for a quicker evolution of your personality'.

PATRICIA URQUIOLA

1961
Graduates from the Polytechnic University of Milan after moving to Italy; she first studied architecture at the Polytechnic University of Madrid
1989
Graduates from the Polytechnic University of Milan
1990-1992
Serves as assistant lecturer to Achille Castiglioni and Eugenio Bettinelli in Milan and Paris
1990-1996
Assumes responsibility for De Padova's new product development office
1996
Becomes head of Lissoni Associati's Design Group and works with Vico Magistretti
1996-2000
Continues working with Piero Lissoni
1998
Enters into partnership with Patrizia Moroso
2001
Opens her own studio in Milan
2015
Is named art director by Italian brand Cassina

'brothers and most of my friends didn't know exactly what they were going to do, but I had a clear goal. So I moved to Madrid, because schools in Asturias didn't offer architecture courses.'

'After three years in Madrid, I moved to Italy. Madrid had become too much of a comfort zone. I fell in love and was open to the idea of going somewhere else. In Milan, they didn't validate all the exams I'd passed in Spain. It was a complicated matter, but at that age everything is easy, you know. It wasn't a problem for me.'

'The teachers in Milan, some of whom were architects, were very good designers. One course was called Industrial Design within Architecture, which didn't exist in Madrid. I became both architect and designer. One of my professors was Achille Castiglioni. He taught me to value the tools for living. Thanks to him, I developed a new attitude. Milan was the perfect place for me at that time. Even though the move was complex, in the end it gave me two professions. I was meant to work in both.'

'A designer is a person who faces problems with an open mind – who solves them in a physical way. I need something that makes me begin to work. If you give me a problem, I tackle it with technology. I'm not a visionary; I become visionary because I *have* to. The input – the problem – amplifies my mind and off I go.'

'Architecture and design go together. Things needed for an architecture project sometimes become pieces of design. Six years ago we were doing two hotels at the same time and we needed handles – in fact, we needed *everything*. One job was a resort in America that required outdoor furniture. Right at that moment, B&B Italia wanted to extend its collection to cover outdoor furniture, so I said: "Here I am."'

'The architectural process is not necessarily longer than the design process. That's important to understand. Sometimes it takes longer to put a piece into production or to optimize a new technique than it does to realize an architecture project – at least at the level of architecture that I'm engaged in, which doesn't include the biggest constructions. As a designer, though, I have less distraction and fewer people to deal with. Architecture is complexity. The level of dialogue is much higher because of all the different materials and technical parts. When I'm working as an architect, I often complain and talk about closing the architecture part of my business and keeping only the small design studio.' [She laughs.]

'Empathy is key when working with different brands. You have to feel and understand the person in front of you, from the inside, even though you arrive from the outside. You have to respect their roots, their heritage – to focus and give it your all. Then you can move from company to company. The dialogue will be different each time. Dealing with different stories works for me. I'm very empathic. I think empathy defines me more than style does. It helps me evolve. I can be in India researching carpets, which are absolutely artisanal, or I can be in Europe working with moulds [for plastic furniture], which are very technical.'

'You need a bit of contradiction in life.'

'I'm not a desk person, I often work standing up or sitting on the floor. After one month in the De Padova showroom, my first job, the boss asked me what I wanted to do with my life. I understood that I was being fired, because I was never at my desk. I said I wanted to work in the technical office. The response was *Go!* – and that's where I spent the next six years of my career.'

'Technicians are essential to the process of design. I was lucky enough to learn this while working at De Padova. Metal, wood, fabrics – we used everything. I also learned to respect and even love the firm's very sensible team of technicians.'

'Working with Piero Lissoni was interesting because he designs for many companies – Cassina, Cappellini, Boffi and more. Now acquainted with the technical side of design, I learned how to present myself and to relate to each company in a different way. By the time I opened my studio in 2001, I was known as a serious person who liked to work hard, qualities that may have appealed to clients – like Patrizia Moroso, for example, who asked me to do sofas. Collaborating with her boosted my credibility.'

'The first year I ran the studio on my own, but then I met Alberto [Zontone], my husband, and he soon took over the business side of things, giving me the opportunity to spend all my time working on projects. I hope we can continue like this.'

'I'm a very inclusive person. My home and my studio are in the same building, because the studio is also part of the family. My daughters find it very natural to live in the same place as my studio. Because everything is connected, I don't waste time. And new ways of working facilitate our lives, of course – not only do family members constantly message one another through WhatsApp. It's also a source of photos pertaining to my projects. I have a chance to approve a design or to make changes, since my team can always communicate with me.'

'I see sensitivity as a democratic quality that is not specifically gender-related. You can't say that men are conceptual and women are sensitive, at least not in my experience. My mother was the more conceptual side of the family and my father, who was an engineer, the more sensitive side. Women are very flexible, very open to change. Women know that if something happens in the family, with the children for example, they have to manage. We practise being adaptable in our jobs as well. That's not a bad thing. We are not insecure about switching points of view or rethinking prejudices.'

'Thinking in terms of goals is a very masculine thing. When I have goals, I keep them quiet. My philosophy is to go step by step and to let things come to me. It's more serene that way. I don't believe in saying that I'm reaching for a specific goal. If you reach it, it's not interesting any more, and if you don't reach it, you get frustrated.' ✕

TRENDS

WORDS *Ronald Hooft*
PORTRAIT *Raw Color*

Dutch architect and columnist Ronald Hooft takes time out for a bit of tongue-in-cheek trendcasting.

A S a professional in the world of architecture and design, you're expected to keep abreast of trends, of course, particularly when you write a column for a leading design publication. Type 'interior trends' into Google and you get more than 23 million hits: countless websites eager to provide you with information. With this in mind, I spot an obvious opportunity to poke a bit of fun at trendcasters. People who call black the new white one year and – you guessed it – proclaim just the opposite a year later. But it's not that simple.

Still and all, why not give it a try? Now that we've entered a period of guarded economic recovery – following more than half a decade of one recession after another – it's about time to consider a permanent departure from that oh-so-safe greige. I can close my eyes and envision a return to cheerful pastel tints: ashes of rose, egg-yolk yellow and pistachio. In chalk paint or as crackle-glaze tile. At the same time, a major Mondrian retrospective at the MoMA in New York promises to bring back primary colours in a big way.

Continuous wars in the Middle East and Africa, accompanied by an endless stream of refugees, will trigger society's longing for handcrafted, locally sourced products. Deep in my bones I feel the revival of macramé, lace curtains, crocheted bedspreads and artisanal ceramic vases. Consumers – burdened by a sense of guilt? – will begin furnishing their homes with ethnic products and prints in the form of hand-knotted rugs, goatskin poufs, and hand-hammered bowls of brass and copper.

Sustainability is translated not only in the use of triple glazing and complicated heat-recovery systems, but also in the application of materials that become more beautiful with age, such as marble, especially when they feature wild colours and patterns: think turquoise and pink, cobalt blue and translucent green. Picture Las Vegas brothels from the 1970s, and combine that image with shoddy materials like chipboard and corrugated cardboard. For an interesting contrast.

The 'hipster trend' is about to experience a definitive breakthrough. Plaster will be chipped off the walls of many through-lounge suburban homes, and bicycles will hang from brackets in the living room while former bike-storage sheds are converted into mini sausage factories or craft-beer breweries. Early adopters are sure to respond with traditional solutions. We'll see a significant comeback of thatched roofs, cork wall coverings and herringbone parquet flooring

In the field of architecture, brick is going to be *big*, but I also foresee a demand for titanium and a huge call for bamboo, not to mention Corten steel. More and more skyscrapers will go up (and up), even though most people can imagine nothing better than owning a detached house. Mountains are poised to become the new beaches, South America is set to be the new Africa, and yes, white will be the new black. ✕

After seeing sensational colours leaking from Ohio's numerous abandoned coal mines, John Sabraw was inspired to develop works of art.

POLLUTION AND

With paints derived from the toxic run-off that pollutes Ohio's coal-mining country, John Sabraw used a simple technique to achieve the ecological complexity of his *Chroma* series.

WORDS *Jane Szita* **PORTRAIT** *Louise O'Rourke*

THE PAINTER

Although producing paint from toxic run-off is relatively simple, Sabraw says it's 'hard to make a viable, consistent and stable pigment'.

BORN in England, artist John Sabraw was still known as a realist painter when he horrified his agent by producing *Chroma*, a series of circular abstract works. Made with pigments derived from the toxic run-off that pollutes the coal-mining region of Ohio (Sabraw is an art professor at Ohio University), the pieces underline the theme of environmental activism in Sabraw's work: he once devised a carbon-offset scheme for artists, which he applied to Leonardo's *Mona Lisa*. Sabraw and chemist Guy Riefler, his paint-making partner at Ohio University, have big plans for pollution-based pigments as a means to clean up industrial sites.

What inspired the idea of making paint from pollution? JOHN SABRAW: Ohio has over 4,000 abandoned mines leaking lifeless but dazzlingly coloured mineral streams. I was struck by the amazing colours and wondered if I could work with them. I quickly discovered that environmental engineer Guy Riefler was already using the run-off to make paint, and he asked me to join him.

Is making the paint a simple process? It's easy – but making a viable, consistent and stable pigment is hard. We start with containers of polluted water, which vary enormously from site to site. We consulted a paint manufacturer in order to achieve a finer grind and the right pH balance to mix with linseed oil or acrylic compounds.

How do you make the *Chroma* works using these pigments? I lay a sheet of aluminium flat, draw a circle and apply lots of water-based pigment to it, creating a large bubble on the surface. Then I wait for it to dry. It takes weeks and weeks. A piece measuring about a metre across has around a gallon [3.79 litres] of water on it, with surface tension holding it in place.

How many of these pieces have you made? There are lots of failures. I've made 30 to 40 successful ones, and the process is evolving and becoming crazier. I am now working on a bigger scale, almost 2 m in width, and I'm doing an experimental piece that's over 3 m wide. The larger the scale the less control, and the more an ecology-like complexity emerges.

Where do you see the *Chroma* project heading? We've just submitted a US$750,000 proposal to make a pilot plant. We want the paint-making process to be commercially viable, and initially we're looking for funding from the university, the state or coal companies. The same process could be used for other polluted sites. It's an exportable technology that could clean up an area in a generation.

Are you involving other artists? I'm making a large batch of acrylics and oils from the heavily polluted Oreton site. Later, I'll send tubes to artists around the world. Their works will form a future exhibition.

What do your *Chroma* works represent? The initial idea was to find an organic way of representing tree rings. These days I begin each work with an idea of something like algae.

Is art important in tackling environmental issues? The science is compelling to those who can process it, but art can connect with people on a more basic, emotional level. It raises awareness and involvement.

How can artists and scientists work together effectively? I've worked with astrophysicists before and now with Guy, and I really like collaborating with scientists. These days, everything is so specialized that there is little discussion among disciplines. But artists and scientists communicated closely in the past. Often, they were the same people. There is a commonality. ✕

johnsabraw.com

'IT'S AN EXPORTABLE TECHNOLOGY THAT COULD CLEAN UP AN AREA IN A GENERATION'

Partners privately and
professionally, Rianne Makkink
and Jurgen Bey inhabit an
intricately intertwined world.

Visit Studio Makkink &
Bey in Rotterdam with
the digital magazine

OUT OF THE

**From dawn till dusk, Jurgen Bey and
Rianne Makkink of Makkink & Bey
make every day count.**

WORDS *Maria Elena Oberti* **PORTRAIT** *Marte Visser*

ORDINARY

JURGEN BEY: Our day begins at around 7 a.m. Rianne is usually up by 6:30. She likes to take her time in the morning and do work around the house. Our mornings look pretty different. Rianne likes to have breakfast at home, usually muesli with tea. She'll read the paper or turn on the television or radio for some noise if I'm not there. We rarely have breakfast together during the week. I'm always on the go. I just grab something on the road, on my way to the train or at the gas station while I stop for fuel – wherever. The city is my kitchen. If there's one thing I need in the morning, it's a shower. It's where I think and meditate. My days don't have much structure to them, but the shower gives me an opportunity to let my mind wander before the calendar starts. If I could, I'd start every day with a 30-minute shower. But that's not always possible.

Our studio is about ten minutes from our apartment. I go by bike or by tram if I'm working from the office, but if I'm going to Amsterdam, I drive. You're expected to move quickly when you're by car, and I find that stressful. The train takes a lot more time, but sometimes I enjoy the slow start. There's nothing to worry about, it is what it is. You're not rushing to win time.

We moved studios just over a year ago. We're on Marconistraat now, near the port in Rotterdam. It's a small office with a huge warehouse attached to it. Our studio has always looked like a warehouse. There are things everywhere, packed and unpacked. It's our way of working. This is the first time we have something closer to a traditional office. I prefer to work out of the storage space. We have everything there, our models, prototypes, all we've ever done. It's almost like an exhibition space. We're always surrounded by our history.

Rianne likes to work with plans and drawings, whereas I work with models. I need to see things in 3D. My worst nightmare is a blank sheet of paper. Some people like to start with a blank slate, but I hate it. That's why I like our storage space and why I prefer to work together. I want as much around me as possible. Working from home is the ultimate pleasure, because everything is there, always. I like to work surrounded by books, with the television or the radio on, with lots of things happening all at once.

We don't have a daily life or a night life. It's not like we go to work and then come home to something else. Our lives are so intertwined. It's hard to tell the difference between work and private life, where work begins and where it ends. It's just our reality.

Our life is not organized. Sure, we have meetings that give some structure to the day, but no two days are the same. Our routine is not having a routine! The only ritual we have is lunch. The whole office sits down together around a big table. I'd say our life is like a television show; you turn it on and it starts running. When it's over you switch it off and you go to sleep.

We both travel a lot. I only need the bare essentials when I travel, I like the idea of having and needing nothing. Rianne travels with some necessities. You'll usually find her with her cape (her shield) and thermos in hand. I don't need much, maybe just some clean knickers. I love to travel. It's where I learn the most.

Our weekdays are pretty hectic. We might work and live together, but the reality is we don't see each other much. During the week we live in our apartment in Rotterdam. On the weekends we go to our house in the countryside. Rianne usually cooks dinner during the week. I cook on the weekends. We only have two burners in our apartment in Rotterdam, so dinners are pretty simple when we're there. On the weekends we put in the effort to eat a proper meal, with real ingredients. Rianne's sister brings us organic meat from her farm. That's what I trust. Otherwise we'll have something from our own land. We have a lot of chickens and roosters there.

Unwinding? What's that? If I had to choose, I'd say Netflix. I like stepping into someone else's world. Everything disappears. Rianne will cycle to relax, or make tea. We usually finish up at the studio at around 7 p.m., but it really depends on the day. We try to be in bed by midnight, but if it were up to me, I'd never sleep. I never want to stop. ✕

**In collaboration with graduates of DAE, Makkink &
Bey presents WorkScape Theatre, an installation on
the future of the workshop at the Bi-City Biennale
of Urbanism and Architecture, now being held in
Shenzhen and open until 4 March 2016**

BREAK
IT
DOWN

GARDEROBE

KOMPOST

Items from the F-abric range are displayed on the walls of Freitag's Grüngasse store in Zurich.

Photo Leandro De Stefani

Daniel Freitag reveals the story behind the compostable F-abric line of clothing.

WORDS *Will Georgi*
PORTRAIT *Mirjam Kluka*

TO many, the name Freitag is synonymous with sustainability, thanks to the company's flagship product: messenger bags made from recycled truck tarpaulins. But Daniel Freitag, who founded the company together with brother Markus, wanted even more. 'We believed that Freitag could become a brand, not just a branded product, by extending the feeling *behind* those bags to other products or areas.'

Over the course of countless brainstorming sessions devoted to exploring possible directions, one idea slowly crystallized: a new 'tarpless' approach that would mean the abandonment of the firm's iconic truck tarpaulins in favour of a new clothing range designed (initially) for Freitag factory workers. 'Sustainable fashion is nothing new – and it's far from impossible to find a good pair of trousers,' admits Freitag. 'It's not easy, however, to find clothes that match our set of values as well as our expectations for the materials and the places in which they're produced.'

While dabbling in a new field did offer Freitag creative opportunities, it also opened up a sizable can of worms. Working with a different material meant the company had to relinquish the successful 'reduce, reuse, recycle' production process behind its popular messenger bags

(*Frame* 105, p. 196). 'We thought all we had to do was find a good fabric, work out a good cut, and produce everything close to where we work,' says Freitag. 'We gradually realized, however, that it was much more complicated than that. Material with an "organic approach" wasn't enough; we needed something that would tick all the boxes.'

What followed was the creation of an entirely green life cycle for the new product line, which started with sourcing fabric in Europe and included a reduced carbon footprint in terms of travelling distance. 'We wanted fibres that could grow in Europe without the use of excessive pesticides and that were also factory-proof: long-lasting yet good-looking. Last but not least, they had to be fully biodegradable.'

His third demand represents an important distinction. Three months after the first pair of trousers landed on the compost heap, everything but the garment's polyester thread had disappeared – 'biodegradable' doesn't necessarily equal 'compostable' – but that wasn't good enough for Freitag. The company then sought out a new compostable thread to complete the loop. 'Perfection is a long process,' he says. 'There's always room for improvement. We use as few chemicals as possible – no bleach, for example – and the final result is environmentally safe.'↳

Markus and Daniel Freitag get (more than) knee deep in a Normandy flax field – one source of the raw material for F-abric.

Photo Lukas Wassmann

'WE CALL THE PRODUCT "CLOTHING" RATHER THAN FASHION'

↰ Now hanging in stores, the F-abric range – composed of hemp, flax and Modal, a beechwood fibre – raises an intriguing question: does Freitag consider sustainability or fashion to be more important to the project? 'Both. Some colours are hard to produce, and we use low-impact dyes, so there are limitations in that sense. But we just heard that one of the shades – industrial green – has been named *the* fashion colour for this season. Luckily, we're on trend. It's interesting to see what's going on in the fashion world, but it's better to find your own style and way of working than to try and be something you're not. That's why we call the product "clothing" rather than fashion.' The latest F-abric development is the first pair of compostable jeans, for which Freitag designed its own denim twill from bast fibres.

What's certain is that the Freitag brothers see 'the product' as just one element of a bigger picture. Sustainable manufacture is not the end of a product's life cycle. 'The first trousers that came from the production company were delivered in a plastic bag. It wasn't "wrong", but it felt that way, because of all the energy we'd spent eliminating the tiniest trace of polyester from the clothes.

That's when we realized that we had to insist on biodegradable packaging, too.'

There's one notable exception to the otherwise fairy-tale ending to F-abric's cradle-to-cradle story: the button on each pair of F-abric trousers. It's the only part of the range that isn't biodegradable, which is exactly the way Freitag wants it. Specially developed by the company, the button (patent pending) can be unscrewed and removed from the garment. Freitag proudly points out that it will probably outlast everyone who buys the trousers. 'We're communication designers, not only product designers. We know how important it is to deliver a story. The beauty of our bag is that it's made from a unique material and tells its own story. A pair of our trousers can't do that. When I wear them, I don't think about anything apart from the fact that they're comfortable. But when I fasten this special button, it reminds me that there is something different about them. That's why we invested so much time in a simple button – to trigger our customers to think about every step in the life cycle of a piece of clothing.' ✕

freitag.ch

FRAME Follow the Freitag brothers on their F-abric-making journey with the digital magazine

WHEN YOU PUT BETTER THINGS IN, YOU GET BETTER THINGS OUT +

MAKING LIFE BETTER AT WORK is about enabling the hidden potential in everything – in you, your organisation and the world around us. Pure materials without unnecessary chemicals, combined with cutting edge ergonomics, leads to a healthier, happier and more productive team. We call it **THE BETTER EFFECT.**

NEW PERSPECTIVES ON SCANDINAVIAN DESIGN

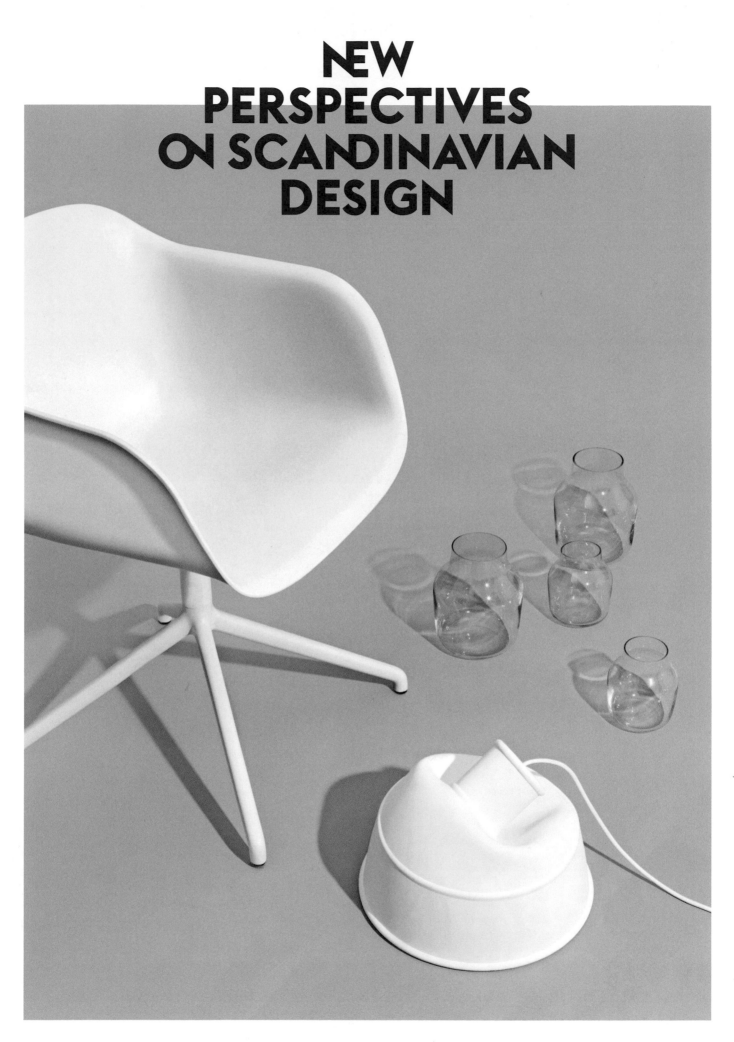

MUUTO

New Nordic

URBAN ACTIVISTS

Partisans may be known for its small-scale projects, but the Toronto firm's ambitions embrace the girth of the city.

WORDS *Elizabeth Pagliacolo*
PORTRAITS *Caitlin Cronenberg*

Offering users scenic views of
Ontario's Georgian Bay – and Lake
Huron in the distance – Grotto Sauna
features a digitally carved interior.

Alex Josephson (middle), Pooya Baktash (right) and Jonathan Friedman (left) pose amid their Gweilo lights.

'BEAUTY EMERGES WHEN DESIGN MISBEHAVES'

'I FEEL a little less stressed these days,' says Alex Josephson. We're sitting at Bar Raval, a small restaurant on College Street in Toronto. The interior is wrapped in CNC-milled mahogany panels that curve to hug every corner. Josephson and his team at Toronto-based architecture and design firm Partisans created the Spanish tapas spot, riffing on Gaudí-esque Art Nouveau as well as muscles – the concept drawings included illustrations of sinuous tissue. When it opened last February, locals fell in love with the place as much as with the pintos it serves, catapulting Partisans' reputation and earning the outfit more clients. In contrast with the studio's residential projects, Bar Raval is publicly accessible. 'When the general population can visit your work, it's different,' he says. 'You're no longer seen as a paper tiger.'

Josephson acknowledges 'a lot of ego in architecture. You're constantly struggling to shape your identity.' In the case of Partisans,

that identity reveals a ballsy, outspoken firm. Over the course of a two-hour conversation, Josephson delves into the ideas that drive Partisans, while also taking aim at everything from derivative Toronto modernism: he mentions Will Alsop's 'masterpiece' – a reference to the British architect's tabletop on coloured stilts for OCAD University, 'which is inevitably a child of Archigram' – as well as native son Frank Gehry, the man responsible for renovating the Art Gallery of Toronto (2008) and, more recently, for realizing new Facebook headquarters in Silicon Valley. 'Zuckerberg hires Gehry? How conservative.'

In its first three years, the studio has completed a wide range of projects, including Bar Raval and Grotto Sauna, another digitally carved beauty with a topographic interior based on a 3D scan of its island surroundings. Meanwhile, the firm is engaged in a years-long revamp of the interior of Union Station (the Grand Central of Toronto), while meeting

with potential clients in places as far-flung as Warsaw, New York City and Los Angeles.

Although landing commissions is high on its list of priorities, Partisans has been interested in big theoretical concepts from the beginning. Now in their early 30s, Josephson and the somewhat mellower Pooya Baktash, cofounder of the company, met as graduate students at the University of Waterloo School of Architecture in Ontario. They each took a defiant approach to the obligatory master's thesis. Josephson focused on Islamic architecture, rethinking Mecca and designing a temporary mosque. Baktash explored the myth versus the reality of Los Angeles, even though he grew up in Tehran and has never set foot in LA. Their shared subversive streak – 'the idea of resistance to the status quo, scaled from zero to infinity', according to Baktash – shot through the ethos of their nascent firm, christened with a name befitting a political movement and eager to push spatial concepts and computational technologies. ↳

The sculptural walls of Bar Raval, a restaurant designed by Partisans, are CNC-milled mahogany panels.

'THERE'S A LOT OF EGO IN ARCHITECTURE'

↰ Enter the Partisans manifesto, which encompasses storytelling, play and collaboration. Its boldest statement: 'We believe that beauty emerges when design misbehaves.' This mind-set allows the team to cast its sights beyond architecture to embody art, activism and urban concepts. 'Architecture is more than buildings. It's also a dream,' Josephson says. The main target of Partisans' avid attention is Toronto, a place Josephson and Baktash hope to change for the better. As they know, however, young experimental firms have been largely left out of the biggest game in town: condo development, a recurring subject in the firm's burgeoning literary output. *Suburbylonia*, a 2014 graphic novel that satirizes the city's building boom as a lost opportunity – citing a vertical suburbia of unimaginative towers sucking the air out of street life – ends with three future-forward ideas: The Genetic City, Urban Podiums and Crazy Towers.

The first would redraw political boundaries so that districts with similar demographics and desires could band together and initiate unexpectedly daring building projects. If this makes the staff at Partisans sound like policy wonks, the second and third ideas flesh out what such structures might look like. They reimagine 'frighteningly formulaic' podiums as zany activators at street level, with Ferris wheels, M.C. Escher-style stairways and webbed structures. Towers rising from these platforms have ambitious new silhouettes that redefine the skyline.

Partisans' critique of Toronto is threaded through other endeavours as well. Examples are the company's After School talk series; its shortlisted entry for the 2016 Venice Biennale (the Canadian pavilion rebranded as a condo sales centre, a tower of scaffolding rising above it); and *The Rise and Sprawl*, an upcoming book coauthored by Dutch architecture critic Hans Ibelings that puts Toronto's condo-ization in a global context.

Partisans' perspective on the city is also central to a Josephson initiative, Art & Architecture Residency Toronto (AART), which he explains later at the studio, a scrappy HQ in 'shared coworking space' MakeWorks. There we find partner Jonathan Friedman and narratologist Nicola Spunt concentrating on various projects: a vacation home, a neighbourhood study, and a restaurant that may or may not feature a knob in the form of a 'giant toy' clearly visible to passers-by. Twisting the knob raises and lowers the building's rolling façade and roof. 'Buildings should perform as public art,' says Spunt. That's where AART truly shines. Developers adopting this proposal can fulfil their public-art obligation – often a simple sculpture plopped down in front of a building – by contributing to an endowment and donating one unit to an artist chosen through an international competition. 'Why not create a legacy by bringing a multidisciplinary visionary here for a year to weave myths about Toronto?' Josephson asks. The idea has garnered support from major art institutions, developers and city council members, who seemingly turn a blind eye as the radical young Partisans blithely hack the town's conservative condo game. ✕

partisanprojects.com

deep space

Design Kati Meyer-Brühl

brühl □
bruehl.com

'Typical office chairs are limited to a certain place,'
says Todd Bracher. 'Trea can live anywhere.'

OUT OF OFFICE

We're working anywhere and everywhere –
a phenomenon Todd Bracher had in mind when
designing the Trea chair for Humanscale.

WORDS *Shonquis Moreno* PORTRAITS *Andrew Boyle*

'**YOU** actually *wear* this chair more than you sit on it,' says Brooklyn designer Todd Bracher. He's referring to his most recent design for New York office-furnishings label Humanscale, which won the Red Dot 'Best of the Best' Award. Trea features a two-part contoured shell that needs no mechanical adjustment and is the product of explorations into exoskeletons, the articulated gauntlets and tectonics of medieval armour, the pelvic bone and the lobster shell. The common thread among these is that they all move in harmony with the living tissue they frame or shelter. 'To make a chair, you need a seat and a back, but how do you connect them in the most efficient way possible?' asks Bracher. With Humanscale engineers and moulders, he sought a design aesthetic driven by efficiency and need – and nothing more.

Trea lacks the myriad knobs, levers and dials often associated with task chairs – but that is precisely the point. Instead it's a multipurpose chair that responds like a carapace to the weight and recline of each sitter. It could be paired with a small table in a hotel room or even commute home with you after work and serve as a dining chair. 'Why can't a dining chair have a slight recline? Typical office chairs are limited to a certain place,' says Bracher. 'Trea can live anywhere.'

In theory at least, the days of taskmasters and beehives are past. We're working more collaboratively. We work standing, leaning, eating and checking Twitter. Static chairs are fading. We're mixing spaces for work and play, answering mobile phones over dinner and ordering Marni dresses at our desks. We're also working from wherever (on the planet) we find a connection. And we're learning that being in any kind of motion throughout the day is healthy. Humanscale has known this for some time. A nimble player in the contract sector since 1983, the brand has teamed up with talents like ergonomics master Niels Diffrient to foster worker wellness, substituting gravity and body weight for easily breakable mechanisms that are unintuitive to operate.

'The office is getting simpler, easier, more adaptable, less expensive, more flexible, more democratic,' says Bracher. 'Open plan has taken over, and at the same time there's been some pushback. A lot of players don't quite know where it's going, but in the next five to ten years we'll see something new. The office as our dads knew it is gone, but the new office has yet to take shape.'↳

'THE NEW OFFICE HAS YET TO TAKE SHAPE'

Trea is a multipurpose office chair that responds to the weight and recline of each sitter.

An invisible recline mechanism makes the underside of the chair as sleek as its 'face'.

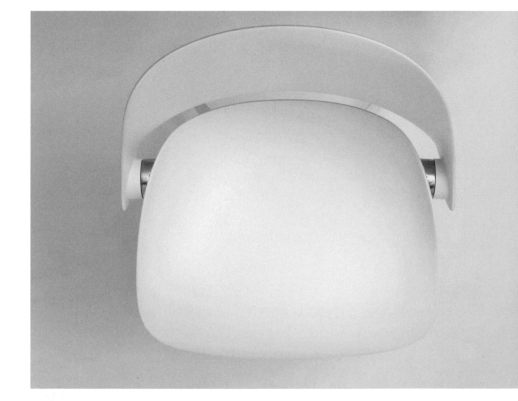

HUMANSCALE

Website humanscale.com
Established 1983
Number of employees 1,000
Headquarters New York, London, Hong Kong
Product range Ergonomic products that improve health and comfort at work: self-adjusting seating, sit/stand desks, monitor arms and task lighting
Bestselling products Diffrient World Chair, Freedom Chair, M2 and M8 adjustable monitor arms
Collaborating designers Todd Bracher, Don Chadwick, Niels Diffrient, Michael McCoy, Mark McKenna, Peter Stathis
Market Worldwide

Bracher's chair is designed to feel as comfortable at the dining-room table as it is in the workplace.

↰ Bracher – a Pratt Institute graduate who studied interior and furniture design in Copenhagen – is an unusual hybrid of businessman and international creative. He returned to New York in 2007 and set up his office in the Brooklyn Navy Yard several years later. He has headed up Tom Dixon's studio in the UK and creative-directed luxury Scandinavian brand Georg Jensen. He counts 3M, Pearl Lam, Fritz Hansen, Cappellini and Burberry among his clientele. He embraces the notion that he is working for the end user and in the service of commerce, and is just as comfortable decrypting the needs of a client who doesn't know what he wants – but thinks he does – as he is with near carte-blanche assignments.

'There's a macro-trend,' he says. 'Everyone wants things cleaner, simpler, more intuitive. But simplicity is a dangerous word. Many things may look simple, but none of them really are. A good example is an aeroplane: the wing is beautiful, but it's about fluid dynamics and structure and material; it has nothing to do with looks. This kind of logic drives a lot of design today. Another example I use is a tree. A tree is the result of a context; it's a product of its ecosystem. You don't say that one tree is nicer than another. Based on this logic, your designs are authentic and truthful. You don't have to question their aesthetics.'

Bracher's logical approach to the design of Trea led to an invisible 'solid state' (no moving parts) recline mechanism the size of a thick hockey puck made from dense rubber and aluminium. 'You need to use the mechanism, but you do not need to see it,' he says. 'If you turn your phone over, it's perfect, clean. No screens, no tubes. It's resolved. All aspects of Trea needed to be resolved.' A pivot – springless, silent and durable – allows the backrest to mimic the natural rotation of the hip. The more you extend the slope of the seat, the greater the recline. The sitter can tilt up to 12 degrees, but a big man won't 'bottom out' and a small woman still gets a good lean.

Today's typical office worker might sit at her computer for 20 minutes, wheel over to a colleague's workstation and eventually return to her desk to eat lunch. Such activities are unwieldy when seated in a standard office chair. 'It's weird to leave your workstation with your task chair. It's like using a bulldozer to go grocery shopping,' says Bracher. The Trea – at the same price point as a static chair – lets you experience various environments, including the home, using one vehicle. 'This isn't a 24-hour chair. It's not what I think of as a call-centre chair. We call it a multipurpose chair, because the workspace has become multipurpose.' ✕

FRAM∃ The digital magazine divulges the development of Todd Bracher's Trea chair

Seated in the Favela chair by Fernando and
Humberto Campana, Norah Stone poses with
husband Norman under the watchful eye of
Alex Israel's *Self-Portrait (Swimming Pool)* (2014).

California residents Norman and Norah Stone attribute the slow rise of design collecting to a lack of great galleries.

WORDS *Anne van der Zwaag* **PHOTOS** *Jeff Singer*

THE FAMILY STONE

I FIRST met Norah and Norman Stone in June 2015. We were in the intimate lobby of Hotel Julien, a boutique hideaway in Antwerp, where I welcomed the trustees of the San Francisco Museum of Modern Art (SFMOMA), who had gathered for a tour of the finest Dutch and Belgian art and design collections on offer. The couple stood out immediately, not only for their distinctive colourful style, but also for their knowledge of the international art and design scene.

A few months pass, and here I am, seated at the Stones' vintage Scandinavian dinner table in Napa Valley, California. Built in 1887, their whitewashed timber farmhouse is surrounded by a vineyard that is part of the property. The landscape alone would be stunning enough, but I'm looking through a window that frames an enormous infinity pool with an intriguing white cube at the centre. It's the work of James Turrell, one of my heroes. As an art-history student in the Netherlands, I could only dream of Turrell's *Skyspace* pieces. Norman and Norah have one in their own back yard. And what better title for it than *Stone Sky*? Elsewhere on the premises, Bade Stageberg Cox Architecture transformed a hillside into what the Stones refer to as the Art Cave. It's all part of Stonescape, their estate and the most unexpected exhibition space I've ever encountered.

The Stones' primary residence isn't this Napa farmhouse, however, but a San Francisco home designed by architect Arthur Brown in 1927. Two very different homes in two very different places, but both are filled with well-picked, carefully arranged pieces from the Stones' internationally acclaimed collection of art and design. Among the works are those by Hans Bellmer, Mike Kelley, Andy Warhol, Gilbert & George, Donald Judd, Bruce Nauman, Richard Serra, Robert Smithson, Theaster Gates and Ai Weiwei. What strikes me is the tale behind each piece they own – stories that illustrate their unique approach to art and their cherished relationships with many of the makers.

The quantity of work on display is impressive, but it's just a drop in the ocean; the Stones' collection comprises around 1,000 pieces. So when – and how – did it all begin? 'In the early 1980s,' says Norah, 'we began collecting modern European paintings. When we joined the Collectors' Forum of the SFMOMA, we made a shift. They asked if we were interested in contemporary art.' Norman finishes the recollection: 'We said we were, but that we didn't understand it.'

'During the mid-1980s,' says Norah, 'we travelled with John Caldwell [former curator of painting and sculpture at SFMOMA], visiting art fairs, museums and collections the world over. He initiated our education in contemporary art, and through him, in 1989, we met art adviser Thea Westreich. We continue to learn from Thea, who's always on the lookout for works of art that complement or are relevant to our collection. When we ask for something, she finds it. She knows countless artists personally, and it's Thea who connected us with Cindy Sherman, Jeff Koons, Richard Prince and others. We're now friends with a number of these artists.'

'We do prefer to see and develop an appreciation of the artist's work before meeting them, though,' says Norman. 'Liking the artist might make us like the work more. We don't want to be influenced in that way.'

The art I see in Napa Valley and San Francisco is conceptually and visually strong, as well as a bit provocative. What does that say about the core focus of the Stones' collection? Norman confirms that a good many of the pieces have a conceptual basis. 'If the idea behind a work doesn't move us, we quickly lose interest. We buy art that really speaks to us, which might not always be visually appealing to the masses.'

'We're very proud of the works that deal with issues such as gender, sexual identity, race and aggression,' says Norah. 'One of our first major pieces is by Joseph Beuys, who was – and still is – hugely influential for contemporary artists. Yes, we may find his installations beautiful, but our respect for him as a human being is even ↳

'DON'T EVER CONFUSE YOUR COLLECTION WITH YOUR EGO'

Norman and Norah Stone commissioned James Turrell to create *Stone Sky* (2005-2006) for their property in Napa Valley, California.

Despite being filled with notable 20th-century art and design pieces – including work from Keith Tyson, Cheyney Thompson, Finn Juhl, Hans J. Wegner and Piet Hein – the Stones' living room feels decidedly homey.

more important. We have to feel something when we look at art. Otherwise, it's like looking at a beautiful person who's empty inside.'

I'm aware that not many people get the chance to step inside Stonescape. Only a few hundred professionals are invited here each year to view the personal collection. 'It is indeed very personal,' says Norah. 'We surround ourselves with our collection. We reinstall everything periodically, so that we can experience the pieces in a different way.'

'I basically spend my life trying to help other people,' says Norman. 'Collecting wouldn't be meaningful if we didn't have the intrinsic motivation to donate the majority of our collection to museums. We don't take any of this for granted. We feel very fortunate to be able to make these gifts to public institutions. When I was a young collector, John Caldwell gave me the best advice: "Don't ever confuse your collection with your ego." I still take his words very seriously; this collection is not *me*.'

From an outsider's point of view, the pieces appear to have been selected for their relationship to one another. I ask whether the Stones are building the collection according to a clear plan. 'We seldom commission, and if we do it comes naturally, as it did with James Turrell,' says Norman. 'When we acquire new pieces, we always consider what they add to our collection and if they will still interest us a year after purchase. Thea guides us to help maintain our focus. This focus in what many people value about our collection.'

Although modest about the role they play in the development of the SFMOMA, the Stones are linchpins in the museum's enrichment and advancement. 'We constantly keep in mind what we feel would add value to SFMOMA's collection,' says Norah. They purposely acquired work by Marcel Duchamp to complement the museum's Duchamp fountain. 'We're not going to build a museum,' says Norman, 'so we don't need 15 Duchamps.'

The Stones are what I call 'art pioneers'. Do they also collect art as an investment? 'Never say never, but it's not our motivation,' says Norah. 'It's not even something we consider. To be honest, we're disappointed that there's so much speculation in the art market. It seems to be more about money and manipulation now. Some prices don't match the quality of the work in question. Many of the famous artists in our collection were emerging talents when we first bought their work. We were fortunate in our choices. The same goes for designers like Claudy Jongstra, Maarten Baas and Studio Job, whose work we starting collecting at an early stage in their careers. The problem is that there aren't many great galleries specializing in design. That's why collectors haven't caught onto it. Photography had a slow start too, so design might catch up in 20 to 30 years. We buy art, design, photography, one-off pieces, editions and prints. We're not bound by rules. We don't want to hurt or harm anybody, but apart from that it doesn't bother us what people say or think about our collection.' ✕

The Stones are trustees of the San Francisco MOMA, which will reopen to the public with an additional wing and new exhibitions in May 2016
stonescape.us

FRAM3 Let the digital magazine take you on a guided tour of Stonescape

A mix of vintage and contemporary art and design in the Stone's bedroom Includes Marianne Richter rugs (circa 1955), a Legnoletto 160 bed by Alfredo Häberli, chairs by the Campana brothers and a Claudy Jongstra bedspread.

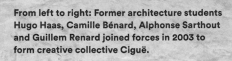

**From left to right: Former architecture students
Hugo Haas, Camille Bénard, Alphonse Sarthout
and Guillem Renard joined forces in 2003 to
form creative collective Ciguë.**

The founders of Ciguë share five pivotal projects that shaped the Parisian collective's image.

WORDS *Maria Elena Oberti* **PORTRAIT** *Fiona Torre*

GAME CHANGERS

Inspired by Hugo Haas's master's thesis, Cabane Morsang was the project that put Ciguë in the spotlight.

Cabane Morsang *Morsang-sur-Orge, 2007*

'We rely a lot on our sensibilities,' says Hugo Haas, one of the four founding members of Parisian collective Ciguë. Driven by a common hands-on approach and their passion for materials, the friends set up shop in 2003 while completing degrees in architecture at École Nationale Supérieure d'Architecture de Paris-La Villette. Since then, the studio has evolved into a professional practice of 20 people. 'The first project that put us on the radar was Cabane Morsang,' recalls Haas, referring to the abstract wooden retreat that emerged from a thesis in which he explored the relationship between the hut and experimental architecture.

A cross 'between architecture and sculpture', the project expresses the group's artisanal approach to design. 'We built everything ourselves, with no outside help. In the beginning, we designed and built all our projects from start to finish: every aspect, including plumbing, electricity and sometimes demolition.' Following instinct and materials found at the construction site rather than drawings, they realized a cabin whose form and structure came out of the process of building it. Despite Ciguë's previous work – custom furniture designs and private residential projects in and around Paris – it was a venture into the woods that put the outfit on the map. 'Cabane Morsang set off the first spark of publicity,' he says. It didn't take long for the phone to start ringing. ↳

Aēsop Le Marais Paris, 2011

↰Cabane Morsang may have given Ciguë the exposure it needed to get the ball rolling, but Haas says that 'what really changed things for us was Aēsop'. The 2011 Aēsop Le Marais project marks the group's first formal encounter with retail. Introduced to Aēsop by Merci's Jean-Luc Colonna d'Istria, Ciguë went on to design a total of seven shops for the Australian cosmetics brand. Ciguë's strategy at the outset was to get to know the company inside out. 'We wanted to get under their skin and to build an authentic story around their products.' With dialogue dictating design, they made the Marais shop a fusion of converging perspectives. 'We blended our input with the Aēsop philosophy, which embodies the interests and values of those who run the company, of course. Think of the result as a system that's been carried into all our Aēsop projects.'

Beyond grasping how to adapt a retail design to the brand it represents, members of the team became real professionals through their alliance with Aēsop, while also being confronted with some fundamental communication problems. 'Tactility and storytelling are really important to us, and it's not easy to explain what you want to do from the other side of the world,' says Haas. With Aēsop founder Dennis Paphitis far away in Melbourne, Ciguë no longer had the luxury of proximity. 'We realized that we had to find other methods of expressing our ideas, such as 3D renderings, schematic drawings, sketches and material boards. We were used to face-to-face meetings with our clients. This was a totally new way of working.'

Since 2011, the year of their first collaboration with Aēsop, Ciguë has designed a total of seven shops for the Australian cosmetics brand.

Photo Emmanuel Barbe, courtesy of Ciguë

Isabel Marant Tokyo, 2012

From Paris to Melbourne, Aēsop eventually led Ciguë to its collaboration with French fashion designer-cum-label Isabel Marant. 'Aēsop Le Marais not only gave us creditability; it validated our competence. We finished the project in July, and by September we were receiving calls for projects – amazing how fast it all happened.' Isabel Marant was one such call. 'We designed four of her shops in 2012 alone.'

A significant period for Ciguë, that year saw Isabel Marant shops pop up in Paris, Hong Kong, Seoul and Tokyo. 'Tokyo stands out most,' says Haas. 'It was our first major project abroad, in a totally foreign country with a totally different culture.' Culture aside, Ciguë found itself having to depend on local craftsmen and builders. 'The start was quite hectic. We were working on multiple projects at the time, and it wasn't easy to manage.' Part of the problem was in Paris, where Ciguë had started to hire more people. 'We developed professionally during the Tokyo project. We learned to be clearer about how we wanted things done, leaving no room for error.' Having studied and worked together since their early 20s, the foursome had established a tight, efficient way of working together, but at that point they 'had to split up, divide the work and, at the same time, open up our creative process to allow other people in'.

The Parisian boutique for Études Studio was built by external contractors, who used scale models and prototypes designed and delivered by Ciguë.

'WE HAD TO OPEN UP OUR CREATIVE PROCESS TO ALLOW OTHER PEOPLE IN'

Photo Tom de Peyret

Photo Koyo Takayama, courtesy of Ciguë

Relying on local craftsmen to oversee the construction of Isabel Marant's Tokyo location, Ciguë continued to gain experience in projects realized abroad.

Études Studio Paris, 2015

While Ciguë continues to work from its core values of materiality and instinct, the outsourcing of production has become an inevitable necessity. Faced with the challenge posed by the demands of an expanding workload and clientele, the collective had to come up with alternative ways of maintaining its hands-on approach. 'We had a bit of an internal crisis caused by an inability to keep making everything ourselves. We wondered how we could preserve the essence of our work – projects that are emotive, personalized and detailed – without the proximity we'd been used to,' says Alphonse Sarthout, another Ciguë cofounder and principal designer.

Reminiscent of Isabel Marant Tokyo, the Études Studio boutique in Paris demonstrates the shift in operations, only on home ground. Designed by Ciguë, its construction was ultimately contracted out: 'We did all the drawings and made the prototypes, but the project was built by others.' As Haas later points out: 'We had to find a way of communicating the details that are so important to those working on site.' Ciguë incorporated the experience gained while working in Tokyo into its plan for Études Studio, providing contractors with elaborate prototypes, samples and scale models. 'We worked as though it was any other international project,' says Haas, 'but now we were in Paris.'↳

Photo Maris Mezulis

Ciguë got back in touch with its roots for the design of Aēsop Rough Trade Nottingham. The team designed and built all elements of the store at its Montreuil workshop and transported everything to the site, where the interior was installed, piece by piece.

'WE WENT BACK TO MAKING EVERYTHING OURSELVES'

Aēsop Rough Trade Nottingham, 2015

↰Since working on the cosmetic brand's display for Merci in 2011, Ciguë has maintained a strong connection with Aēsop. 'They give us a lot of freedom and let us go with our gut,' says Haas. For the Nottingham location, intuition led to a laboratory theme. 'It's a workshop of the future, but with some vintage elements.' Designed in partnership with fellow Parisian and glass-maker Franck Buhot, the entire project was built in Ciguë's Montreuil workshop – 'like we used

to do', says Haas – after which separate elements were transported to the site and reassembled there.

Though time has proved the benefits of outsourcing, these designers ultimately rely on themselves when developing complicated projects. 'We've learned to be selective with our energy. As much as we'd like to, it's not possible to be everywhere at once, building and installing every commission from beginning

to end. We've gone from having to build everything ourselves and learning how things work as students to working internationally with prototypes in order to transmit ideas.' Aēsop Rough Trade Nottingham features a complex system of glass and machinery, all designed by Ciguë. 'It was extremely experimental,' says Haas. 'The project gave us the opportunity to get back in touch with our roots.' ✕

cigue.net

MIX IT UP

Carpet tiles are no longer limited to squares, nor are they reserved for the floor – two themes Ege explores in its flexible Figura collection.

WORDS *Daniel Golling* **PHOTOS** *Brian Buchard*

MANY objects compete for attention in the strict hierarchical system of interiors, but some are more likely to attract admiration and awe than others. The leading roles go to chairs, sofas, tables and lamps – interior objects that aren't ashamed of doing what all good actors do: expressing and exposing themselves. Their designs are the sort we don't only *know* by name, but with which we might even be on a first-name basis; we casually refer to our 'Egg Chair', our 'Parenthesis' or our 'Superleggera'. Like the stars of stage and screen, they depend on a supporting cast. Floor coverings are one of the necessary – and often anonymous – products whose presence we register but rarely *really* consider. They are the extras of the design show.

Anyone involved in the designing, making and (not least) marketing of carpeting might appreciate the metaphor and be acutely aware of the problem it illustrates: how do you draw attention to a product whose purpose, it seems, is to facilitate the leading stars of design? This is the way we've become accustomed to considering carpets, but do we see a change on the horizon? Susanne Lykke Møller, visual communications director of Danish carpet brand Ege, answers with a resounding *yes*.

Ege's latest product, Figura, is a floor-covering concept that Møller believes could be a game-changer. The product range consists of eight shapes, from simple squares to more complexly contoured tiles; each is available in what the company calls '15 qualities'. It's easy to create herringbone-patterned flooring with Figura's square and rectangular tiles. Although squares and rectangles can't be combined with the other seven shapes, the more elaborate forms, like Curve and Wave, can be configured ↳

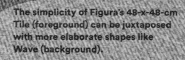

The simplicity of Figura's 48-x-48-cm Tile (foreground) can be juxtaposed with more elaborate shapes like Wave (background).

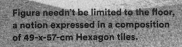

Figura needn't be limited to the floor, a notion expressed in a composition of 49-x-57-cm Hexagon tiles.

↰in myriad ways. Add to this a palette of 370 colours, and you have what Møller describes as 'a playground for architects. We haven't seen carpets with these shapes and forms on the market before,' she says. 'They're more organic than previous carpet tiles, so they give rooms a softer, gentler ambience.' Møller also believes that the almost limitless possibilities offered by Ege's new collection can produce floors with an interesting three-dimensional quality. Figura is a response to current consumer demands: 'For many, the minimalistic look has come to an end.'

Ege, whose history dates back to 1938, is firmly rooted in the values typically associated with Scandinavian design. The notion of what those values are, however, has changed in recent years. Once a haven for minimalism, Scandinavia has begun to reveal an appetite for colour and pattern. After all, it was Danish company Hay that turned Memphis legend Nathalie Du Pasquier into a household name.

Coinciding with Scandinavia's liberation from the aesthetic straitjacket of minimalism is a revolution in laser-cutting technology that has prompted Ege to invest in new equipment for its Herning factory. The brand can now produce shapes that were once impossible. 'You could say that Figura is a response to the urge for individual expression,' says Møller. 'Architects and designers have the freedom to play. Figura is not just a common tile that you lay out on a 4,000-m² office floor. You can use it to make something with a very individual look.' What makes Figura even less commonplace is its backing, which is made from recycled and regenerable PET felt.

Even though Ege's products are durable, the company and its in-house designers don't give too much thought to how long a certain pattern or particular design will last. Trends come and go, and the cycles are getting shorter. Maybe that's one reason why floor coverings have historically dwelled just outside the limelight: once the floor is in place, it *stays* in place. Substituting one chair for another can be done on a whim. Now, however, a floor made from carpet tiles can be just as temporary. 'You can change it overnight,' says Møller. 'You can decide how long you want the carpet to be part of your interior, and the design has so many possibilities. Depending on the colours used, you can turn the volume up or down.'

Not only is there an increased interest in colours and patterns; today's consumer pays more attention to carpets in general. The tried-and-tested sound-absorbing qualities of carpet combined with the ease of use inherent in the Figura line have resulted in new – might we even say 'daring' – interior applications. Tom Dixon's carpet-covered ceiling for restaurant Craft London springs to mind. (Coincidentally, Dixon chose carpets from Ege.) And what's to say that carpets can't be used as wall coverings? We don't have to go back to the tapestries of the Middle Ages for inspiration. In the small museum that's part of Ege's headquarters and plant in Herning, a 1970s advertisement features a framed shag rug hanging on the wall of a living room, complete with heavy furniture from the era. With the introduction of Figura, the carpet may have come full circle. ✕

Photographer Brian Buchard interpreted Ege's Figura in a series of images that highlight the flexibility of the collection

EGE CARPETS

Website egecarpets.com **Location** Herning, Denmark **Established** 1938 **Number of employees** 550 **Annual turnover** €105 million **Area of distribution** UK, USA, Scandinavia, France, Germany, Dubai **Market sector** Hospitality, offices, healthcare, education **Product range** Carpets and carpet tiles **Bestselling products** Highline concept (bespoke carpet designs) **Collaborating designers** Conran and Partners, Nicolette Brunklaus, Christian Lacroix

With eight shapes – each available in 15 carpet qualities – and 370 colours on offer, Figura is 'a playground for architects'.

Harvest

Schemata Architects raises the stock. Es Devlin helps Louis Vuitton expand its fandom. Bonsoir Paris hypnotizes for Hermès. Formafantasma struts its stuff on the catwalk. Olafur Eliasson gets retrospective. ZCD Architects changes it up for Hussein Chalayan. It's the pick of the crop from the worlds of art and design.

Photos courtesy of Bureau Betak

FRAME Watch Bureau Betak's floral affair blossom to life with the digital magazine

In Full Bloom
Bureau Betak *raises the whimsy quotient for Dior's Paris Fashion Week show*

PARIS — We're all familiar with the green wall. Now Alexandre de Betak of Bureau Betak has given us the violet hill. De Betak, scenographer for innovators from Rodarte to Viktor & Rolf, brought spring to autumnal Paris when he was tapped by the House of Dior to produce the show for its S/S 2016 ready-to-wear women's collection.

Dior introduced its A/W 2014 couture line against a canvas of 150,000 orchids; this season's show was another floral extravaganza, a lavish gesture to mark the end of Raf Simons' successful stint as creative director of womenswear at Dior. To match Simons' diaphanous designs in organza and cotton voile, De Betak raised a hillock of delphiniums over the Cour Carrée du Louvre.

Inside its generous hollow, the man-made mound became a white cavern that, though windowless and opulent in scale, had the lightness of a garden gazebo. De Betak sowed additional flowers on a smaller slope raised against one interior wall interrupted by a white doorway through which models appeared to form two *défilés*. Will Paris Fashion Week's most aromatic show inspire Dior's next fragrance? — SM

bureaubetak.com

Photos Michael Najjar

Space Invader

Michael Najjar *takes guests at the Kameha Grand Zurich Hotel on an intergalactic voyage*

ZURICH — Ever since British fashion designer Christopher Kane launched his galaxy-print designs five years ago, many in the industry have been engrossed by outer space. What's been a trend, however, is becoming an invasion. Proof of the phenomenon is the work of German artist Michael Najjar, who was commissioned to design a Space Suite for the Kameha Grand Zurich Hotel. Those familiar with Najjar's life and work know that he is well acquainted with the conditions of extraterrestrial existence: the Berlin-based artist has been training to prepare for his role as one of Richard Branson's Virgin Galactic Pioneer Astronauts. The expedition will make him the first contemporary artist to set foot in outer space. ↳

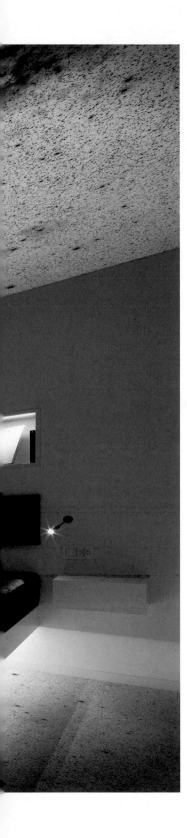

↰ For the time being, Najjar's vision of space takes the shape of a silvery hotel suite studded with outlandish motifs. Interstellar images captured by the Hubble Space Telescope appear on both ceiling and carpeted floors, while a bed – or 'sleeping module' – hovers weightlessly in the corner, seemingly unaffected by the pull of gravity. Greeting guests as they enter the 'space station' is a computer-generated female voice inspired by John Carpenter's sci-fi film *Dark Star*. Additional exaggerated details include 3D-printed rocket-inspired spotlights and an astronaut's wall-mounted glove, which doubles as a shelf as it extends a helping and eerily curious hand. Conclusion: zero gravity, centrifuge training and spacewalk simulation are not necessarily conducive to achieving an effective spatial design. — LG

michaelnajjar.com

An astronaut's wall-mounted glove doubles as a shelf in artist Michael Najjar's Space Suite.

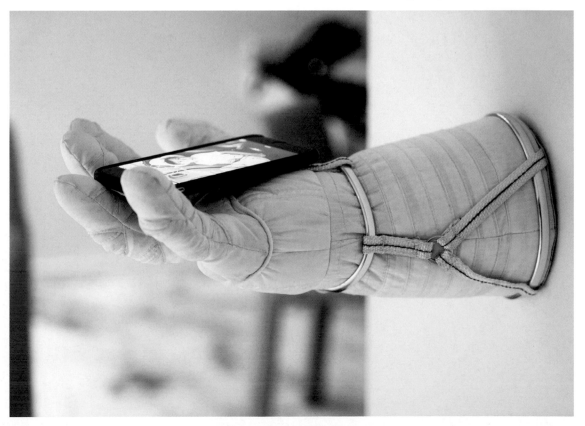

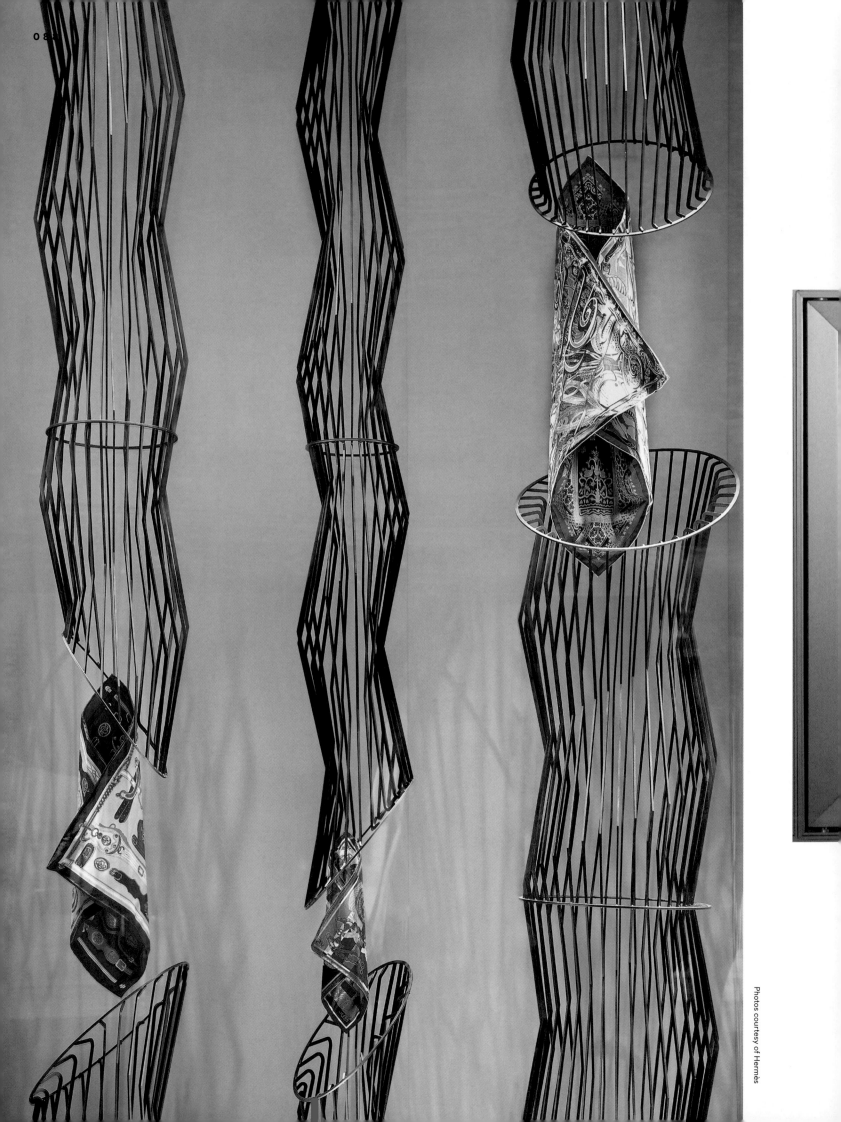

In a Trance
Bonsoir Paris *hypnotizes for Hermès with a series of kinetic* étalages

DUBAI — Referencing kinetic art in its moving window displays for Hermès at The Dubai Mall, Bonsoir Paris placed products by the French fashion house at the centre of each hypnotic composition. The designers – who produced a similarly striking cover image for *Frame* 105 – were responding to the theme of the brand's S/S 2015 campaign: Flâneur Forever.

The engaging displays were intended to catch the attention of passers-by without overwhelming them with superfluous effects. Through shadow play and layering, the basically simple arrangements achieved an intriguing sense of complexity. According to the designers, the window entitled Why Time? invited shoppers to pause and daydream – to lose time and become a *flâneur*, an idler adrift within today's urban fabric, absorbing the sights and sounds of the city while wandering aimlessly. After all, a lazy stroll can be liberating. Picturing the *flâneur* as a radically romantic figure, Bonsoir Paris made the concept part of a modern experience characterized by an abundance of time. — **JP**
bonsoirparis.fr

Photo Arjen Schmitz

Designer Drugs
Maurice Mentjens' *House of Smart* *probes the inner workings of the mind*

EINDHOVEN — Most of us are familiar with the concept of a smart shop. Chances are, a wacky interior radiating with the dazzle of multicoloured florescent lights pops into mind. Add to the equation a flock of tourists sporting Amsterdam-themed souvenir apparel, and the picture is complete. But in Eindhoven – the world's smartest region according to the Intelligent Community Forum – things look a little different.

The House of Smart, yet another psychedelic experience conjured by Dutch designer Maurice Mentjens, attempts to reflect the city's brilliant brainwaves through a surprisingly sober palette. Mentjens, who together with Arnout Visser presented titillating mushroom-shaped lamps at this year's Dutch Design Week, is certainly no stranger to the provocative. Despite the shop's monotint interior, however, the hallucinogenic gestures are hard to miss.

Defining the stripped-back 20th-century space is an intricate web of slender wood beams painted grey. Used as display shelving, the intersecting network evokes the complexity of the nervous system. White neon tubes diffuse an ethereal glow throughout, while the vibrant packaging of the shop's mind candy lends potent punctuations of colour to the neutral backdrop. The result is an almost religious reminder of the mystical power of mind-altering substances. In perfect alignment with Eindhoven's status as *the* capital of intelligence, the store offers visitors an (albeit momentary) escape from the everyday. — NB

mauricementjens.com

Photo Danica C

Over the Rainbow

Olafur Eliasson's *retrospective leads visitors through intersecting realities*

STOCKHOLM — Extending across the exhibition halls of the Swedish capital's Moderna Museet, Reality Machines is a retrospective honouring the visionary poetics of Danish-Islandic artist Olafur Eliasson. A champion in the integration of space, light and colour, Ellasson concocts experiences that combine elegant design with the primitive power generated by larger-than-life natural phenomena. His extensive portfolio includes projects as diverse as film, sculpture and interior design, which often problematize, if not entirely blur, the fine line between artefact and observer, perception and reality.

Although they often target the senses, Eliasson's works are nevertheless grounded by potent philosophical and political ideas. This is most explicit in Little Sun, an LED solar lamp he designed for off-the-grid communities in Africa. Eliasson's refined approach to art reaches its zenith when he tackles physical phenomena in an immersive way, using simple yet provocative elements. One of the Swedish exhibition's highlights, *Seu corpo da obra* (2011), is a labyrinth of colourful semitranslucent panels that overlap to create a shimmering kaleidoscopic world.

As boundaries between architecture and the visual arts disappear, scale and technology become instant crowd-pleasers. Eliasson's prowess, however, lies in his ecological focus and in the sense of wonder he bestows on the natural 'machinery' that influences our perception of reality. — **NB**

olafureliasson.net

Boom Box

Bureau V *pumps up the volume with National Sawdust, a stage for promising musical talent*

NEW YORK — In September, music facility National Sawdust moved into a former warehouse in Williamsburg, Brooklyn. The highly reconfigurable non-profit performance, rehearsal and recording venue – a collaboration between design studio Bureau V and engineering firm Arup Acoustics – is cradled within a concrete envelope that rests on acoustic isolation springs. A synthesis of the finely crafted concert hall and the black box, with its capacity for unconventional programming, the space features finishes that absorb, diffuse and reflect sound, including an articulated precision-movement stage and curtains that help 'tune' the interior to the instrumentation. Architect Peter Zuspan says that open drapes benefit 'reverberant, unamplified performances', whereas closed curtains 'absorb a blast of amplified sound'. Even the hyper-graphical walls have a dual aural purpose: they wrap the faceted two-storey chamber hall and comprise a perforated 'visually translucent but acoustically transparent' metal-and-textile skin. This box-in-box system hangs 46 cm from the factory's exposed brick carapace, says Zuspan, 'so when a semi-truck hits a taxi cab outside, you hear and feel nothing inside'. Artists can even record in the building's black herringbone-tiled lobby. — SM

bureauv.com

Cloud of Coats

Schemata Architects *literally elevates the merchandise for sportswear brand Descente*

TOKYO — Schemata Architects has unveiled a simple yet strategic concept for Descente Blanc, a new line of apparel from one of Japan's leading sportswear manufacturers. Descente is defined by its urban aesthetic – a mix of cutting-edge versatility and sophistication that architect Jo Nagasaka incorporated into the store's spatial identity. Currently, outlets can be found in three Japanese locations: Osaka, Daikanyama (Tokyo) and Fukuoka.

Nagasaka utilized existing materials from the surrounding environment, including timber, which he moved from the exterior into the Tokyo store. Clothing hangs from the ceiling of the raw industrial space on long tubular rails that can be raised and lowered mechanically. These racks display multiple copies of one design, an apparent reference to mass production. The factory feel is reinforced by the prevalence of steel, bare surfaces and neon lighting. Furniture, arranged as if in a gallery setting, injects a thoughtful note that can be seen as a nod – more romantic than critical – to industrial production.

'We focused on redesigning the service process – the routine of shop staff taking items from the stockroom and delivering them to a customer,' says Nagasaka. Storage space integrated into the ceiling, however, compels staff in search of products to move vertically instead of horizontally. — **JP**

schemata.jp

Photo Kenta Hasegawa

Travel Case

A touring immersive brand experience by set designer Es Devlin *helps Louis Vuitton expand its fandom*

LONDON — For a month this autumn, Louis Vuitton's Nicolas Ghesquière translated his 12-minute A/W 2015 ready-to-wear show into a touring installation dubbed Series 3. Covering three decaying floors of 180 The Strand, a brutalist building in central London, the scenography by British set designer Es Devlin (*Frame* 101, p. 148) suggested that although the well-heeled may make luxury brands rich, it's a much wider public that makes the brand. Design houses are finding ways to ensure that rarefied industry rituals are no longer the sole domain of the *haute*

set — that those who don't wear the clothes or attend the shows can experience the collections, too.

'I approached Louis Vuitton and Nicolas Ghesquière as a pair of characters in a play,' says Devlin, whose work ranges from small-scale theatre to Olympic ceremonies and Kanye West extravaganzas. 'My process is to seek a narrative, however abstract, asking not so much how will it look but how will it make people *feel*.'

The installation evoked the autumn collection and show through many media ↳

↰ and material choices, all imbued with 'a little anarchy', which formed a contrast to models who typically move on the runway while guests are assigned (hierarchical) seats. Those attending Series 3 walked around, and models appeared as life-size images on columns illuminated by LEDs.

In 15 scenarios, the team layered narrative elements deftly, and content shifted seamlessly from one medium to another: a white winter 'yeti' coat was accompanied by an auditory windscape in one room, and the adjacent space displayed a snowstorm interpreted as digital snow or 'white noise'. The event often underscored the exchange between craft and concept, past and future at Vuitton. Devlin was struck by the juxtaposition of analogue and digital at the Asnières atelier: lasers and CNC routers

next to simple knives and rulers. She sat two artisans in a room; their hand-making was recorded by cameras and projected onto screens behind them. Devlin talks about a brief that included weaving processes leading to the collection, as well as 'the relationship between designer and artisan, the futuristic inspiration, and the artisanal practices that turn ideas into material'.

The show exposed Vuitton to a different demographic. 'The vintage trunk stickers that people were free to take away are now popping up all over London on the backs of phones and laptops,' says Devlin. 'I love the fact that visitors who might feel too intimidated to walk into a Vuitton store left the exhibition with LV-monogrammed phones for free.' — SM

esdevlin.com

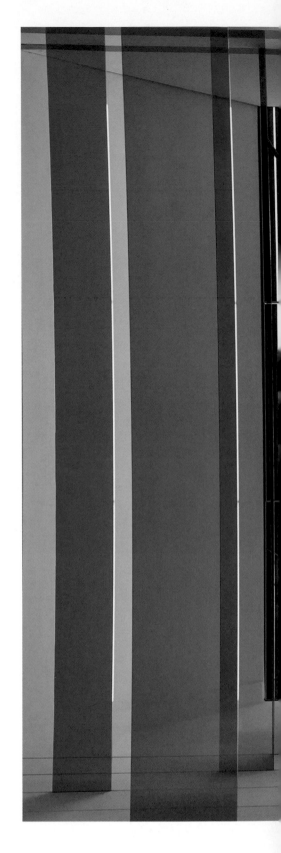

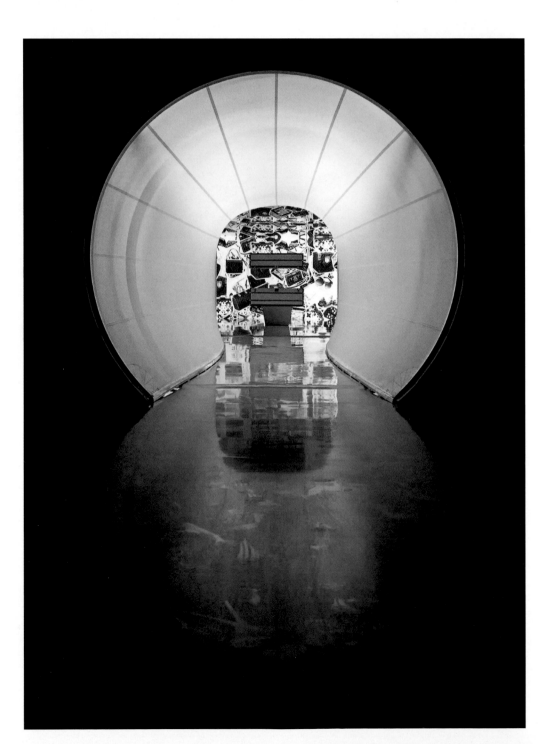

Es Devlin's set design for Louis Vuitton underscored the brand's exchange between craft and concept, past and future.

Polychrome Home
Adam Goodrum*'s earlier design for an emergency shelter is a twinkle in the eye of his latest work*

FRAME Adam Goodrum discusses his work at Melbourne's NGV in the digital magazine

Photo Brooke Holm

MELBOURNE — At the National Gallery of Victoria, three houses sit primly in a row. Shards of light striking the iridescent structures – composed of dichroic-laminated acrylic – feed the overarching shadows behind them. The colour-bending homes, aka Unfolding, scored Sydney-based Adam Goodrum the 2015 Rigg Design Prize, Australia's prestigious triennial award for contemporary furniture and object design.

The title of the work holds its premise. Unfolding was inspired by Goodrum's investigations into flat-pack housing. Each shimmering abode is an extension of the cardboard shelter that Goodrum designed a decade ago as a place of refuge capable of being transported by and released from a helicopter to aid victims of an emergency.

Unfolding recalls Goodrum's earlier concept: a structure that begins as a flat pack of two panels, nested together, which become a house when pulled apart. Though Unfolding may not survive the next cyclone, Goodrum draws attention to the need for emergency shelter through a glimmering wink of refracted light. — LM

Unfolding is on display at the Ian Potter Centre, National Gallery of Victoria, until 7 February 2016

adamgoodrum.com

The Hang of It
Hussein Chalayan's *London boutique ushers shoppers into a different dimension*

LONDON — Cypriot fashion designer Hussein Chalayan is known for creating the extraordinary by taking something banal (a coffee table) and turning it into something equally banal (a skirt) using a less-than-banal gesture (telescopic levitation). Most recently, he came up with shirtdresses that dissolve under a shower of water to reveal evening-wear beneath. We can only hope that Chalayan will one day come up with an entire collection that mutates into, say, a shop featuring clothes from that collection. Until then, London's ZCD Architects are distilling physical space for him.

The outfit's latest boutique, which in true Chalayan fashion can be converted from store to event venue, opened this autumn on London's Bourdon Street; described by ZCD as a 'shop-within-a-shop', the store is defined by a black steel frame. The metal structure both preserves and reshapes the space, while also serving as a hanging rack. Inside are only two other objects: a black boat hull-cum-bench that functions as seating, display unit or dinner table; and a black-lacquered cash counter in which a digital timer marks the passage of time without telling the precise day or hour. A 'threshold zone' at the entrance marked by jet-black floor tiles signals the transition from the street into another territory.

Minimal finishes in black and white reinforce the boundaries of the retail floor while providing a graphical yet discreet backdrop. ZCD didn't want the interior 'to wrestle with' its content for the visitors' attention. Instead of being *mano a mano*, the two fit hand in glove. — SM

zcdarchitects.co.uk

Photo Leon Chew

 Let the digital magazine transport you to the Sportmax S/S 2016 fashion show

Feel the Tension

Formafantasma *maps out space with taut lengths of PVC*

MILAN — Known for its experimental projects and material studies, Formafantasma took to the catwalk to design a set for the Sportmax S/S 2016 collection. To counteract the predominantly grey 20th-century interior of Palazzo delle Poste in Milan, the designers chose terracotta and PVC film in three warm tones as the primary materials.

The design juxtaposed traditional Mediterranean elements – Formafantasma's Andrea Trimarchi and Simone Farresin are Italian – with a contemporary style to put a modern spin on deconstructivism. Plastic film created spatial boundaries: rolls of PVC stretched from ceiling to floor and continued, forming three sections of a looped catwalk. Heavy cylindrical pieces of terracotta provided enough tension to hold the lengths of film in place, offering definition and sharpness to the abstract composition. The catwalk was set at ground level to remove the common hierarchy between models and spectators, who were seated on rows of wooden benches among the narrow translucent partitions.

The impactful yet frugal set highlighted the designers' sense of responsibility for our world's limited resources. And as it was temporary, the project served as a framework that allowed Formafantasma to conduct a 'material study for impermanent spaces'. — JP

formafantasma.com

Float On

Acne's Korean flagship hovers weightlessly amid an assembly of concrete and steel

SEOUL — Designer Sophie Hicks' flagship for Stockholm-based fashion brand Acne Studios in Seoul's Gangnam district sits – gossamer and luminous – in a bed of wild strawberries, crowned with ductwork and lined with concrete. This industrial-ethereal contradiction reflects the area's identity, as well as the contrast between Acne's vocal aesthetic (the name of the label could refer to blemishes but is actually a cheeky acronym for the collective's primary pursuit: Ambition to Create Novel Expressions) and the more retiring aspects of Swedish culture. 'Sweden is a culture of light and air,' Hicks writes, one that values 'modesty and discretion'.

Inside, two floors of concrete poured in rough timber forms float amid – without touching – exterior polycarbonate walls through which daylight diffuses onto freestanding steel garment displays. There is no decoration of any sort and no mechanical equipment, the ductwork that might have threaded the interior having been coiled atop the roof. The consonance of a handful of diverse materials – woodgrain-tattooed concrete surfaces and spiral stair, metal cash counter and displays, and glowing polycarbonate walls – vaporizes into an atmosphere of cool warmth. Hicks, with good reason, calls it 'otherworldly'. — SM

sophiehicks.com

Off Campus

Dutch creative agency Staat *raises the bar for contemporary student life*

AMSTERDAM — During the *belle époque*, the education of wealthy young people included travelling through the Continent, sketching Mesopotamian ruins and learning classical languages. Away for months at a time, the bourgeois backpackers of the era wandered in the company of the *haut monde* and basked in the comforts of Europe's finest hotels. Founded by Scot Charlie MacGregor in the Netherlands in 2012, The Student Hotel – a home-away-from-home for interns, researchers, university students and, yes, travellers who can book for a night, a semester or even a school year – has been reintroducing the concept to a broader audience. It shifts the burden from universities – now landlords as much as educators, but for whom dorm design is a low priority – to a brand able to 'do it right' by exploiting the hospitality industry's recent successes.

MacGregor hired Amsterdam studio Staat (which spells its name ...,staat) to help cultivate and frame an intensely social and intellectual time of life. 'Comfort, convenience and community' shaped the design of signage, interiors, exteriors and architectural elements in 485 rooms in ↳

Photos Kasia Gatkowska, courtesy of Staat

↰ Rotterdam (2012), 707 in Amsterdam West (2013), 309 in The Hague (2014) and 574 in Amsterdam City (2015). Projected for summer 2017, new locations are expected to pop up in Florence, Eindhoven and Groningen. Amenities include 24-hour security, 40-m² kitchens, 1,000 m² of study space and libraries, recreation rooms replete with table-football units, and a restaurant and espresso bar handsome enough to draw a larger public.

   Colour and energy mark Staat's work, which ranges from shop interiors to graphic design. For The Student Hotel, the studio used layers. First layer: furniture forms a variegated landscape of new, vintage and modern pieces. Second layer: dynamic, humorous graphics in the spirit of street-art murals take the place of traditional finishes for interior walls. Bold colour-blocking compositions invigorate communal areas and make 'unexpected colour statements': fields of pink, red and yellow wall one room, while dark-grouted white tile grids the walls of another. Lavish violet upholstery is juxtaposed with whitewashed brick. Carpets in zesty hues indicate social zones and add an extra boost of colour. The third layer consists of enlarged texts: pop-wisdom and 'quirky talking points' printed in a bespoke type. And the bedrooms? Surprisingly, the fourth and final layer is neutral: white walls, wood veneers and slate tiles – a blank page for self-expression. — SM

staat.com

Colour-blocking compositions enrich communal areas in Staat's design for The Student Hotel.

Photos Andreas Keller, Altdorf

Road Trip

Visitors navigated Audi's high-octane 'experience walk' at the Frankfurt Motor Show

FRANKFURT — Asked by Audi to stage its latest range of cars at the 2015 Frankfurt Motor Show, three-dimensional brand specialists Schmidhuber sculpted an 'experience walk'. Rather than being confronted with the full range of Audi automobiles from the outset, visitors first moved through a series of installations. 'We turned the traditional communication principle on its head and showed the advantages of the Audi brand in a new and emotional way,' says Michael Osterstag-Henning, managing partner at Schmidhuber.

The journey began on an exterior escalator that ascended through a mirrored structure composed of hexagonal 'cells'.

Advancing to Audi Technologies, visitors caught a glimpse of the goods through a virtual window, which revealed up-to-the-minute data about the cars' technical specifications. Walls carved from ice in the arctic room embodied the extreme lifestyle of the Quattro rally-inspired car, while streams of flashing LEDs injected intensity into the Audi Sport area, featuring the re-creation of a racetrack.

Did the brand's most experiential exhibition to date whet visitors' curiosity? Audi and Schmidhuber hope so. After all, an inquisitive mind is part of the German brand's DNA. — CW

schmidhuber.de

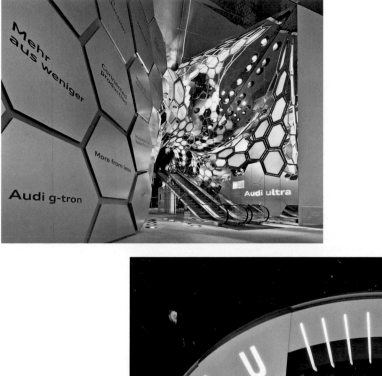

Photo Naho Kubota

Layer upon Layer
Jordana Maisie *piles it on for*
Australian shoe brand Feit

NEW YORK — Founded in 2005, Feit
makes precision-sculpted, no-logo, all-
natural footwear – qualities reflected at
its latest store in New York's West Village.
A canyon-like landscape that stretches from
floor to ceiling was conjured by Australian
designer Jordana Maisie, who stacked
thin birch-plywood boards as if creating
a gigantic layer cake. Air between layers
enhances the feel of lightness, as do irregular
voids that punctuate the display units.

'My immediate response to the site
was a need for the design to extend into the
street and not sit back,' says Maisie. 'It was
important for the store to have a nuanced
optical element that would allow visitors to
see shifts as they move through the space.

I wanted to give each volume a unique
identity on every face.'

Making complex contours was a
challenge: 'We had to ensure that the units
could be manoeuvred by a maximum of four
people and could fit through the door.' Once
mapped and CNC-cut, the modules were
fabricated in a Bronx workshop before being
assembled on site 'like a three-dimensional
puzzle'. LED lights concealed within the
layers can brighten or dim in harmony with
seasonal conditions, particularly the intensity
of natural light on the street outside. The
optical effect is further enhanced by mirrors,
which also help to magnify the size of the
compact 39-m² shop. — JS
jordanamaisie.com

Frame of Mind
Refik Anadol *redefines the boundaries of reality with* Infinity

ISTANBUL — A state of immersion is a state of consciousness in transformation. A bit of a mouthful? Not to worry. Turkish artist Refik Anadol's installation, *Infinity*, offers a window through which to explore the abstract experience of artificial awareness. Presented at Zorlu Center of Performing Arts Centre during the Istanbul Biennial, the mesmerizing space invited visitors into an alien audiovisual landscape created to transgress the normative boundaries of perception.

An elemental part of Anadol's ongoing project – *Temporary Immersive Environment Experiments* – the installation 'questions the relativity of perception and how it informs the apprehension of our surroundings'. To achieve the desired effect, the artist constructs provocative artificial worlds intended to soak the neurons of those who enter his stimulating settings, which deconstruct and rearrange reality.

For the biennial installation, Anadol's concept of infinity determined nonphysical space through algorithmically generated projections and sound. Once inside, the 'immersant' was confronted with a swarm of organic grids and lines that interacted to conjure a 3D pseudo-world. The longer viewers lingered in the environment, the more their minds accepted artificiality as authenticity; the result was a shift of consciousness. In his work, Anadol not only addresses immersion but pushes the boundaries of traditional visual art, inching us ever closer to the shores of the final cyber-frontier. — **LM**

refikanadol.com

FRAM3 Immerse yourself in Refik Anadol's *Infinity* with the digital magazine

Photo Refik Anadol

Anything Goes
A concept shop in Beijing eliminates the elitist view of luxury fashion labels

Photos courtesy of WAA

BEIJING — The refreshing philosophy of Chinese retailer AnyShopStyle holds that fashion is based on personal taste (as opposed to the opinions of industry insiders) and that emerging designers are as good for business as business is good for emerging designers. In brief: exclusivity is out of style. Tasked with designing the brand's Sanlitun concept store in Beijing, local firm We Architech Anonymous (WAA) envisioned a space that would make fashion feel inclusive and would establish 'a democratic space' in which to showcase a rotating roster of work by 300-plus designers and their micro-collections. To display such a large number of labels equally, the glazed floor-to-ceiling store front was cleared of imagery, signage and branding, thus placing the focus on the apparel alone. Because it is impossible to anticipate all the colours of designs that will sweep through the shop, the backdrop defining the interior was rendered in a high-contrast but limited palette composed of peach, camel and midnight blue – each borrowed from *Untitled (50°54'37" N, 4°24'26" E) 9"*, an oil painting by Belgian artist Pieter Vermeersch. The shop's large planes of colour and hyper-graphical forms are balanced by the bareness of their surfaces, resulting in a strong canvas on which to present the collections.

WAA turned the interior into an abstracted Platonic landscape with the aid of basic geometric shapes: triangles represent the earth and circles the sky, while squares outline the details (clothes) of daily life. A centrally positioned display unit consists of chamfered triangular blocks of engineered quartz. Stacked unevenly, these appear to cascade before flattening into a field of triangular floor tiles that form an irregular pattern, suggesting an outcropping of rock. Around the unit, a lavender carpet carves a jagged path through the terrain. Garments are framed by perforated metal and illuminated Barrisol wall panels, and spare brass hanging rails run almost the length of the room. Sliding doors, also made from perforated metal, conceal fitting rooms and cash desk. Overhead, surveying it all, another sheet of Barrisol surrounds a large circular ceiling fixture that provides diffused and seemingly natural light. Inside this shop, a new day is always dawning. — SM

w-a-a.cn

Summit of Parts
Daisuke Sugawara's *plywood mountain-scape both divides and connects a kindergarten interior*

Photo Jérémie Souteyrat

MISATO — Located in a residential neighbourhood one hour's drive from Tokyo, Yutaka Kindergarten features classrooms that surround kids in what looks and feels like a mountainous landscape. The school was designed by architect Daisuke Sugawara, who responded to a brief that asked for a learning environment which would nurture children to actively develop their own personalities and to socialize with others regardless of age. Rather than confining pupils to one room, the rectangular building facilitates movement and participation. Six classrooms are arranged around a common area where children of different ages play together.

The use of partitions makes the individual rooms feel almost like a single space. Cut-out panels of layered plywood form the silhouetted foothills and slopes of mountains whose peaks help to support the ceiling. The mountain range dips down to 120 cm at its lowest height — high enough for children to be immersed in their own world yet low enough for staff to keep an eye on adjacent spaces. Glossy ceilings reflect activity happening 'over the fence', urging curious kids to investigate. — KH

sugawaradaisuke.com

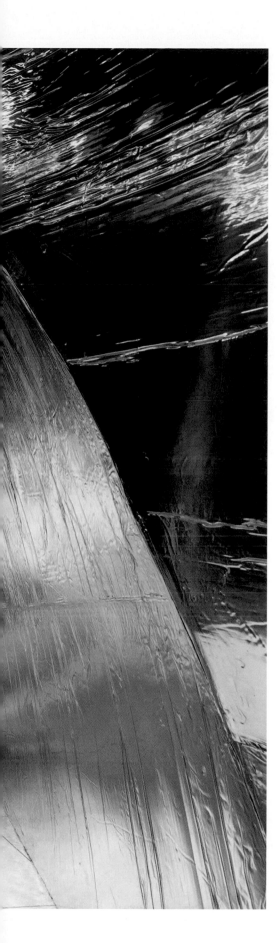

Wrap Party
*Past and present collide
at Miu Miu's S/S 2016
presentation*

PARIS — During Paris Fashion Week in October, Miuccia Prada once again tapped AMO, the research branch of Rem Koolhaas's Office of Metropolitan Architecture (OMA), to frame its S/S 2016 runway show. AMO's solution involved the insertion of an arching, brutalist construction into Auguste Perret's rigid and monumental Palais d'Iéna. To define the path taken by the models while providing a background for the fashions, AMO designers threaded the aqueduct-like structure through the building's hypostyle hall, alternately hiding and revealing its columns and forming the abstraction of a 'timeless ruin'. The insertion's squiggling mass, both voluptuous and sharp-edged, was in stark contrast with the blunt linearity of the architecture around it. Unlike the decay of a ruin, however, the installation was well clad with aluminium thermal insulation in three gold and silver finishes: bubble wrap, smooth and corrugated. Ranged roughly parallel to AMO's bright ruin along the perimeter of the hall, the audience enjoyed a long view of Miu Miu models meandering fluidly in and out of the catwalk. — SM
oma.eu

Skin Deep

*The fast pace of the fashion world
informed the adaptable surfaces in
Hannes Peer's interior for Iceberg*

MILAN — 'The shop that changes its skin – that's the main concept behind it.' Hannes Peer is referring to his design for Iceberg's 250-m² Milan flagship, whose launch coincided with the city's September fashion-week events. Embodying the quick turnover of fashion, rotating triple-faced billboards flick from mirrored and marbled surfaces to Olivier Zahm's photography for the latest Iceberg campaign.

Not only can the brand's campaign-related artwork be updated each season; the billboards' remaining two faces can also be replaced over time. Peer envisions filling the shop with colour, with text-based art à la Chris Wool, or with depictions of inspiring interiors. 'The outcomes are limitless.'

Marble may *still* be all the rage, but that's not why Peer picked it. 'I actually chose to work with high-definition *imagery* of marble rather than the physical material. I'm portraying it as a form of contemporary pop imagery. Like Andy Warhol presented his icons, I wanted to use the image of marble ↳

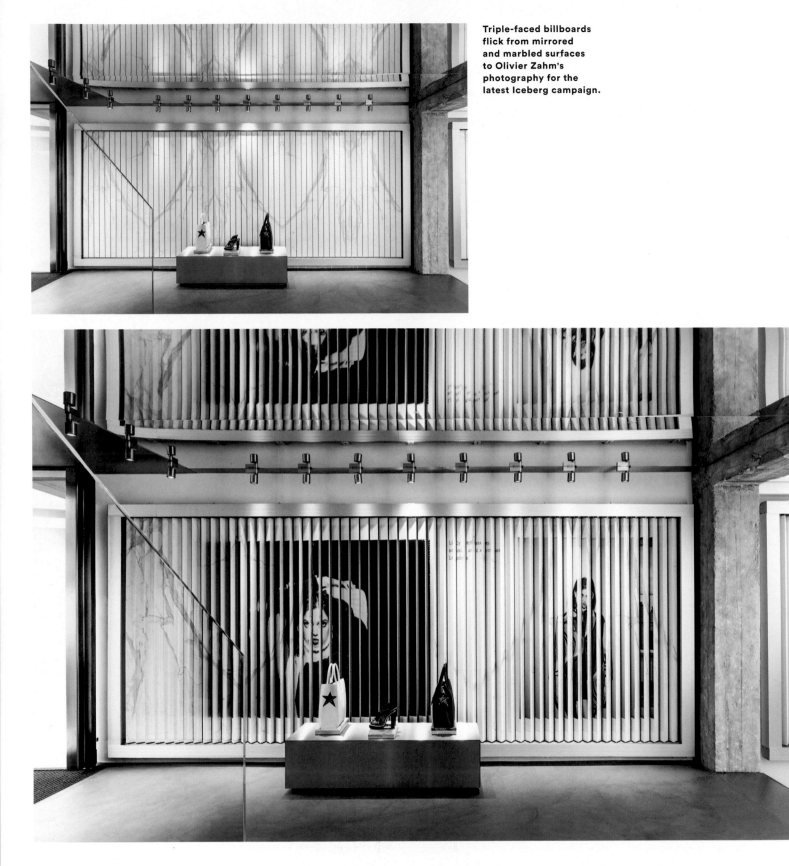

Triple-faced billboards flick from mirrored and marbled surfaces to Olivier Zahm's photography for the latest Iceberg campaign.

↰and what it represents today – luxury and pop – in a subtle and ironic way.'

The only 'real' marble features on tabletops made from *marmo bianco statuario*, which contrasts with the aluminium concert platforms that function as displays. 'I find it interesting to create these kinds of contrasts within a single space,' says Peer, 'to use industrial aluminium elements and combine them with the most precious marble available.'

Iceberg underscores Peer's vision of future fashion-house flagships as one-off spaces for experimentation. 'Each should be different and unique in its own way, with at least one new idea that sets it apart from its predecessors. Flagship stores should represent their brands, but they should also be very special shopping experiences. I think Iceberg's Milan flagship is a big step in that direction.' — TI

hannespeer.com

W

W I N D O W
M A N N E Q U I N S
F R A N C E

e v o l u t i o n
i n s p i r a t i o n
r e v o l u t i o n
i n n o v a t i o n

the designer's mannequin

www.window-mannequins.com

MAKE MOVE

All set to open London's new Design Museum, director Deyan Sudjic discusses the institution's future and the changes affecting design today.

WORDS *Jonathan Openshaw* PORTRAITS *Mate Moro*

'London is becoming Europe's closest thing to Shanghai,' is how Sudjic explains the changes his city is experiencing. 'Yes, it's exciting, but it's also consuming itself.'

DEYAN

If you believe in the metaphoric power of architecture, then comparing the Tate Modern with the Design Museum can tell you a lot about the place held by art and design in our lives. The thrusting, phallic, industrial grandeur of the Tate is impossible to ignore, whereas the Design Museum is housed in a former banana warehouse tucked away in a quiet corner of London that few people actually go to. Contemporary art is the charismatic *enfant terrible* of our times, whilst there's still a sense that design is encumbered by its function, made mundane by its usefulness.

The situation may be about to change. This year the museum will make its long-anticipated move to the former Commonwealth Institute in West London. Restored by John Pawson, the listed building is over three times the size of the current Shad Thames premises. It's a move that has dominated the tenure of the museum's current director, Deyan Sudjic, who took over the role from Alice Rawsthorn in 2006 and has spent much of the last nine years raising £78.5 million in funds for the move and wrangling planning applications.

Playing the long game is a strength of Sudjic's and indeed seems to define his approach to the directorship and to design in general. A trained journalist and editor, he founded the cult title *Blueprint* in 1983 before going on to edit *Domus*, the Italian *grande dame* of design. He continues to be a prolific author today, recently publishing *B is for Bauhaus: An A-Z of the Modern World*, as well as a monograph on Italian architect Ettore Sottsass, and this cerebral attitude sets him apart in a digital landscape that demands pithy soundbites of no more than 140 characters.

Sudjic is still having his portrait done when I arrive at the museum, so I'm ushered up to an empty floor lined on one side with floor-to-ceiling windows looking out over the river. The only objects in the room are a couple of small chairs and a side table set with two glasses of water. 'Sorry, this isn't very welcoming, is it?' says Sudjic, laughing as he walks in and sees the setup. 'But this room is where we started out, you know. The whole team was on this one floor.' It's obviously a fitting place for the interview.

We're sitting here in London in mid-October with the Frieze Art Fair raging all around us, and it's a reminder of the remarkable transformation art has undergone in the last few years. Everyone seems to have an opinion on art now, whether you're eight or 80. The same can't be said of other creative disciplines, such as design and architecture, but do you think this could be changing? DEYAN SUDJIC: Well, yes and no. Art speaks for itself and is good at creating this very direct kind of shock and awe that has proved so popular in recent years. The Tate Modern's Turbine Hall is a masterclass in the democratization of art, with huge commissions such as Olafur Eliasson's postapocalyptic sun or Louise Bourgeois's spiders. These works really don't need a caption; just being present is enough. And design is not about that. Design does need a context; it needs to frame something. The point of the Design Museum is actually to tell the story from the perspective of the user – the maker as well as the designer. It's not a one-way conversation. So for me design has this kind of schizophrenia: it's sometimes about answering questions and sometimes about asking them. I went to an extraordinary Frieze Art event at Sotheby's earlier this week, which was part art auction, part disco. Hundreds of beautiful young people were clearly there for the circus around the art, rather than for the art itself. There's a sense of disgust amongst a certain strand of the art world around what's happened in recent years, with the market being transformed and distorted by the power of money and celebrity.

And it's significant that London has been the melting pot for a lot of these changes. Just looking out at the skyline from the Design Museum, which is dominated by the Victorian Tower Bridge set against a backdrop of controversial additions – like Rafael Viñoly's Walkie Talkie – I'm reminded of the pace of change the city is going through. There is a residual belief that London is a gentle, conservative place where nothing very much happens. But we need to wake up and recognize that we are living in a time of ruthlessness, and London is becoming Europe's closest thing to Shanghai. This skyline was in fact explicitly patterned on Shanghai, planned during Ken Livingstone's tenure as mayor. The idea was to turn the city into a financial capital. But it was done in a very literal way. He wanted a city that *looked* like a financial centre, and in those days that was Shanghai. London is starting to look like a three-dimensional architectural advertisement for a city. Yes, it's fantastic, and yes, it's exciting, but it's also consuming itself. Housing has been a catastrophe, and people can't afford to live here, which will kill things off pretty fast if we let it go ahead.

So you're saying there's a surface-level idea of what a modern city should be and how it should look, but less of an engagement in the support structures and systems you need to have in place to make it happen? My work with the Urban Age Project is based on the idea that cities are not made by planners, architects or developers – they're made by people, and often these people despise each other and are locked in personal skirmishes. Making a city is an extraordinary thing, and the lasting question for me is: can you actually make one? Or is urbanism a bit like meteorology, in that you can observe it closely and make predictions, but you can't actually make it rain?

The Designs of The Year exhibition at the museum has become a good way of tracking our changing sensibilities. It offers a snapshot in time of our material culture. It's interesting that whilst our lives become increasingly digital, there's also a growing interest in connecting with physical spaces, materials and how things are made. We're living in the age of mass extinctions caused by the digital world. These things [gesturing to my iPhone] have killed off so many other things: cameras, telephones, maps, libraries, newspapers. But I think what comes alongside that is an opposite impulse for solid things and materiality. Think about vinyl records, which are showing an increase in sales percentage year after year, or niche magazines with no hope of a sustainable business model, and yet they still exist. Maybe this has something to do with the maker movement and a need to connect with how things are created. Design is certainly changing, and so is our relationship to objects. But this has always been the case and is what makes design so fascinating: it is a direct response to the changing conditions that we find ourselves in.

What is the role of the museum today? We're living more and more through screens, yet the act of getting together in one space seems to be more important than ever. Instead of losing ground in the digital age, the institution seems to be retrenching. To do this job, I draw a lot on my background in journalism. Although I probably chose a very good time to leave print journalism, the fundamental idea of storytelling and taking a point of view is more important than ever. There's a lot to be excited ↵

'DESIGN HAS THIS KIND OF SCHIZOPHRENIA : IT'S SOMETIMES ABOUT ANSWERING QUESTIONS AND SOMETIMES ABOUT ASKING THEM'

D
E
S
I
G
N

D
U

J
O
U
R

Deyan Sudjic selects five ideas that reflect today's zeitgeist

1 JASPER MORRISON'S SIMPLE PHONE FOR PUNKT
'This very elegantly designed phone (*Frame* 107, p. 224) is smart enough to leave us alone when we want to switch off from work.'

2 GRAND THEFT AUTO V
'Neither movie nor game, it introduces a new cultural form. It also reflects on the dematerialization of the world and the remarkable speed with which new products can spread; in this case millions of purchases were reported the first weekend after its release.'

3 VINYL DISC
'We are still hungry for material objects and the analogue world.'

4 GOV.UK
'The British Government had the courage to shut down dozens of individual government websites and condense them all into one clear, easy-to-use site – its most powerful form of communication with its citizens – that allows people to make a will, apply for a passport, register to vote and pay their taxes. The one

visible piece of traditional design is the use of Margaret Calvert's font, Transport.'

5 AUSTRALIAN CIGARETTE PACKAGING
'Carefully created design that does its best to persuade us not to buy something, this packaging is meant to be unappealing in colour, imagery and typeface. It's good design by being bad design, though I hear that it's boosted sales of cigarette cases.'

Even as the world becomes increasingly digital, Sudjic sees the emergence of an opposing appetite for solid things and materiality.

DEYAN SUDJIC

1952
Born in London
1976
Graduated from Edinburgh University with a degree in architecture
1983
Cofounded *Blueprint* magazine
1992
Published *The 100 Mile City*
1996
Appointed director of Glasgow's Festival of Design
1999
Director of Glasgow UK City of Architecture and Design
2000
Editor of *Domus Magazine*
2002
Director of the Venice Architecture Biennale
2007
Appointed director of the Design Museum
2008
Published *The Language of Things*
2016
Opens London's new Design Museum

FRAME Watch a time-lapse film of the Design Museum's construction via the digital magazine

↰ about in contemporary design, and it's easy to get caught up in the excitement. *Wired* is a great magazine, for example, but it's also very into the wow factor, without necessarily having the critical distance needed to look at the consequences of the innovations it features. I guess the role of an institution like ours is to try and have it both ways: to engage in the excitement of the now, but to take the critical distance granted to an institution.

It feels like the fast-forward button has been pressed on our lives. Everything is short form, immediate. It's about the now and the next, but it's often hard to rise above that babble. A good example is 3D printing, which has generated an explosion of interest in recent years that seems out of proportion to its actual significance. Just as the microwave didn't replace the kitchen, the 3D printer isn't likely to replace the design studio. How can you filter out the hype and cut to the core of what is important in contemporary design? Of course there's a lot of surface froth, and you need to respond to that, which is why we do the Designs of the Year to take the temperature of our times. But I'd say that manias over things like 3D printing are mostly quite harmless. It's the bigger shifts that are more of a concern to me, such as the observation that when Instagram was bought by Facebook for US$1.5 billion, Instagram had 12 employees. Compare that with Kodak, which operated in a similar space but created 80,000 middle-class engineering jobs for life. So yes, it's exciting to see whizzy self-driving cars, but we need to ask: what are the implications? Will they put delivery drivers and taxis out of a job? And the answer is: yes, probably.

The Design Museum is also on the edge of massive change and upheaval, moving from the Shad Thames site where it's been since the late 1980s and taking on an ambitious new site at the former Commonwealth Institute in Kensington, West London. What's behind the move? When we set up here in Shad Thames, it was a wasteland. It has been the most remarkable journey for the area, and the East is very much where London has been moving during those years. But there are also limitations for an institution like ours. It's only 3,000 m², and it's about 15 minutes from the nearest tube station. The location does limit the audience, and once you get to the museum, there isn't enough to keep you active for half a day. Ever since I took on the directorship we have been planning the move, and we finally settled on the former Commonwealth Institute, which is a building I remember from my youth. It was built in an early 1960s explosion of brotherhood, equality and all that stuff, with each of the 54 member states making their own diorama. The Australian booth showed you how to sheer a sheep, whilst the Sri Lankans unfortunately shot a tiger and stuffed it. So it has this quite interesting history, but the building has really fallen into a state of disrepair, with the concrete roof rotting away. My first thought on seeing the space was 'this is impossible', but there was also a real desire to return the building to its former glory as a cultural institution.

And so an open competition was held for its restoration, with the most obvious names associated with large-scale public projects in the running, including David Chipperfield. But you finally settled on John Pawson, who hadn't done a major public commission before. Why Pawson – and what is your aim for the new space? I think part of the role of the

'THE ROLE OF AN INSTITUTION LIKE OURS IS TO ENGAGE IN THE EXCITEMENT OF THE NOW, BUT TO TAKE THE CRITICAL DISTANCE GRANTED TO AN INSTITUTION'

museum is to use your commissioning power to make things happen that otherwise wouldn't. John is a fantastic talent, and he had something to prove in a way that David probably didn't. His is a relatively small practice when compared with David Chipperfield Architects, so we got a lot of his time. John understood the brief from the start, which was to preserve the original qualities of the building whilst tackling some of its quite serious issues. The Commonwealth Institute has the most amazing spatial qualities but, as a product of its time, was built with poor-quality materials. The interior is lined with something called 'wood wool', which has the same relationship to architecture as tinned Spam has to cuisine. The traditional approach to conservation doesn't apply here, so we had to consider carefully what to preserve and what to replace at each stage. The end result is fantastic, however, and what John's done is to produce a building that is actually far better than what was there originally. It will allow us to continue our work on a much larger scale, with studios for designers in residence, learning spaces, a lecture theatre, a library, an archive – it's a place that can really come alive and have the sense of a working, thinking community. ✕

designmuseum.org

eve table base
for iPad mini & iPad Air

WORK IT OUT

Offices fit for the future

Many companies tossed out cubicles a long time ago. The idea was that open-plan offices would generate cross-pollination among staff. Times have changed, and many employees no longer work in a fixed environment. It's time for interiors to play catch-up, a topic we break down in this issue's Frame Lab. We discover *how physical space affects creativity*, hear about *Studio O+A's human-centric design approach,* and list *five steps that can lead to future-proof offices*.

From the Inside Out

KURSTY GROVES KNIGHT AND OLIVER MARLOW DISCUSS THE LINK BETWEEN PHYSICAL SPACE AND CREATIVITY IN WORKPLACES.

WORDS *Floor Kuitert* **IMAGES** *Akatre*

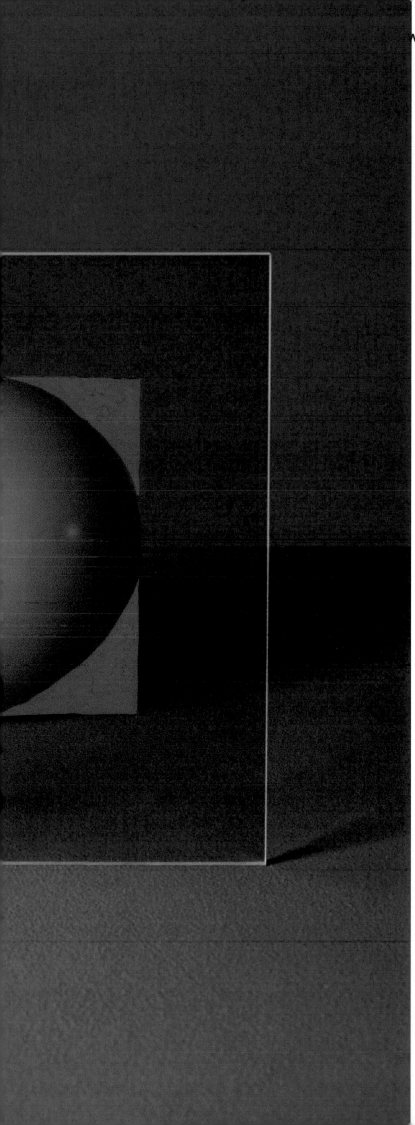

'**THE** conversation around the impact of the physical environment on workplace behaviour has grown over the past few years', says Oliver Marlow, creative director of design practice Studio Tilt. 'This has been aided by the changing nature of the way we work and by the increasing importance of creativity in many industries.' He has found, however, no resource that is extensive or conclusive enough for use in building environments that specifically stimulate creativity.

Marlow is part of a research team that includes writer and innovation consultant Kursty Groves Knight, the IE School of Architecture and Design, and Impact Hub GmbH. They were commissioned by UK innovation charity Nesta to explore how a physical space can enhance our ability to think creatively and, subsequently, to be innovative.

Groves and Marlow sit down to exchange views on the most significant themes that define the outcome of their in-depth study.

The understanding of creativity has changed

KURSTY GROVES KNIGHT: A growing number of organizations view creativity and innovation as important for the future of work. Previously, creativity wasn't synonymous with business; it was a concept reserved for artists. There's been a shift in the value of terms like 'design' and 'creativity', which are now seen by many as ways to enrich life, but also to benefit companies.

Creativity in business was once a solo endeavour, but that's changing. It's no longer about the lone inventor or the advertising genius. Over the last ten years or so, people have started to understand that creativity is a collaborative, social activity. The more you're able to unite different perspectives, bounce ideas around and get stimuli into the process, the better the outcome will be.

OLIVER MARLOW: There's also a growing awareness that creativity is essential for innovation. The ability to think differently – or to approach a problem from a different perspective – is at the heart of creativity. As a designer, I believe that everyone is inherently creative from a young age. The construction of their working life often doesn't let them express it, though. If we understand innovation as the ability to put creativity to use – whether in terms of developing new constructs or different models and products, for example – we can question why it has become such a key component for businesses, and thus for the working landscape.

KG: We need to innovate in order to survive – let alone prosper – and businesses are acutely aware of that.

Physical spaces and social settings have a huge impact on people's productivity

KG: Our surroundings, the spaces we inhabit, influence how we feel and align. If people are aligned, they feel that they have the freedom and autonomy to explore. And by exploring different possibilities, they are better able to develop a forward-thinking attitude.

OM: If you look at the history of work, you'll find that almost everyone worked at home or close to home. Work wasn't separated from the rest of a person's life. Separation came with the Industrial Revolution: you had a place where you worked and a place where you lived.

We understand the challenge involved in such changes, but workspaces still shift from extreme to extreme – from cubicles to open plan to pods to lounges – rather than following designs by people with an insight into *how* people operate. There's lots of quality research and knowledge – whether science-based or intuitive – about which context works best for different people and about the socio-dynamics associated with group creativity. Today we focus on component elements of space, each of which lends individual autonomy to that space while, at the same time, allowing for the ↳

↰ development of an overall identity or footprint that represents a particular organization.

KG: Since the birth of the office, there have been one or two standout examples of office buildings designed to support a workflow. I'm thinking specifically of Frank Lloyd Wright's Larkin Building, designed in 1903. Certainly in the last 100 years, though, office space has been treated as a kind of commodity, an efficiency-driven facility. Traditionally, physical space has been seen in terms of overhead costs and not as a strategic tool that leverages human performance. There's been a big shift in that mind-set. The idea of space as a strategic tool is not new to designers, of course, but it is new to organizations that have been driven by financial matters.

Today's co-working spaces express an aesthetic of empowerment and freedom

OM: Certain examples that we researched afford both autonomy and community. Look at co-working spaces, whose aesthetic has developed into a recognizable language. Originally, co-working was born of a need to step away from any form of traditional workplace and, in so doing, to provide users with completely new surroundings.

KG: I think part of the success of co-working is aligned with the basic needs of creative environments. In part, they are a reaction against the staid old supertankers of the corporate world, which run on fear and bad coffee, whereas co-working is all about freedom and great coffee. We could all be working from home, but people are sociable creatures.

There's just something about the empowerment to choose where you want to work and with whom. Part of the aesthetic of co-working – raw materials found or thrown together, objects seemingly handcrafted – sings to values that are the antithesis of

those that underpin the machine-made look of the traditional office, with its cookie-cutter grey Formica, suspended ceilings and fluorescent lighting.

Current trends are an extreme reaction to the traditional office

OM: People talk about the denaturation of traditional workplaces – about today's spaces being the lowest common denominator in an effort to suit as many people as possible without contravening health and safety regulations.

KG: Yes, and the big trends we've seen – open plan, cubicle, hot-desking and activity-based work – have all been introduced en masse as a reaction to other ideas that simply don't work. Many, in an attempt to find a quick answer, take the shape of over-the-top offices that mark the other end of the extreme. Every room is different, playful and imaginatively depicted. But in the end, the phenomenon is nothing more than a response to the depersonalized office.

OM: As mentioned earlier, space is a tool – an instrument that an organization can use to help form its corporate identity.

Offices designed to nurture out-of-the-box thinking don't have to look like giant playgrounds

KG: There's been a huge war for talent, which has resulted in an external expression of what today's creative organization should look like. But the success of new office spaces emerged from both an understanding of

'The workplace is a *solid reminder* of a company's decisions and values'

intense, productive teamwork and a perception of our need to leave such areas of fierce concentration in order to disengage from a dynamic situation. Unfortunately, the implications led to the conclusion that offices should look like giant playgrounds, which I think is quite naive, but I also recognize an increasingly sophisticated notion of what a creative environment should encompass to help people perform.

Physical space can chart an organization's growth

KG: It's good for people to see progress by observing a company's premises. A start-up, operating on a shoestring and forced to make do, differs from a business that's going through a growth phase and needs flexibility and room for expansion, not to mention a more mature organization that wants its physical space to express stability and a certain level of success.

OM: A natural trajectory of institutionalization evolves over time. Take the coffee shop, for instance. So much happened in and around London coffee shops in the 17th and 18th centuries. Some of the activity was serendipitous, of course: the right people being at the right place at the right time resulted in the right atmosphere. It's as though we've come full circle.

KG: I think we're going to see smarter organizations giving equal weight to physical spaces, staff, operations, services, products – after all, the workplace is a solid reminder of a company's decisions and values.

We're holistic beings. Our workspaces should follow suit

KG: Our research-backed experiments add to our previous experiences. Among the things we now know to be true – and important to human productivity, concentration, performance and creativity – is the use of natural light. One of the more fundamental truths is the human need not only for time alone but also for social interaction, two requirements that

have to be present in workplaces that set aside roles for creativity *and* a well-designed space. We've learnt about basic elements like texture, material and colour, but such things cannot be treated as isolated factors for the improvement of performance or creativity. We're holistic beings.

A space is as creative as the people who use it

KG: Most often it's our less tangible, more cultural surroundings that can make or break success. You can have a beautifully designed physical setting but an absolutely rotten culture: usually an unfavourable combination. Conversely, you can have a quickly thrown together office and a tight, positive culture that add up to a winning concept. What needs to be addressed first is the idea of a corporate culture that is supported by a physical workspace. Rather than looking to aesthetics and stylistic shifts as ways to solve organizational problems, a company should begin by attending to its office culture and the needs of its staff.

Future workspaces will be designed from the inside out

KG: I see people in the years to come considering what workers need to do, how they need to interact, and how they need to behave in a given space. From there they move to a design that takes into account how workers ought to experience the corporate culture, the brand, the business. It's a reversal of the more traditional way of designing. Instead of creating a space and putting people in it – those annoying creatures that mess up my beautiful environment – I imagine organizations and designers working together, putting staff first and designing from the inside out. ✕

nesta.org.uk

Spaces for Innovation, a book to be released by Frame Publishers in the spring of 2016, is based on Nesta-commissioned research into the link between physical space and creativity in workplaces.

Business or Pleasure?

Photo Jasper Sanidad

Boxy comfort zones at Uber 11 offer employees temporary relief from the hustle and bustle of the office floor.

EVEN THOUGH MOST OF ITS CLIENTS ARE FIRM BELIEVERS IN THE POWER OF TECHNOLOGY, STUDIO O+A DESIGNS ONLY HUMAN-BASED WORKSPACES.

WORDS *Giovanna Dunmall*
PORTRAITS *Jeff Singer*

BASED in San Francisco, Studio O+A is the go-to practice for some of the biggest tech innovators in the world: clients include Yelp, Facebook, Uber, Cisco Systems, Open Table and Samsung. In *Ten Typologies*, a publication that is part guide, part manifesto, the studio lists the spaces a contemporary workplace needs in order to function properly. These include the 'library' (a designated area for privacy), the 'town hall' (a central gathering space, often a multipurpose kitchen with several access points) and the 'shelter' (a tentlike structure that cloisters but doesn't remove staff from the action). 'When a workplace is too sterile or formal, people are less inclined to share ideas, to socialize with each other,' says Primo Orpilla, cofounder and principal of Studio O+A. Technology may have made it possible for us to work remotely, but 'the office as a physical space isn't going anywhere', he says. Not only is it a rallying point for colleagues to gather; it also

reflects your company's values. 'It tells people what your company is about, philosophically and sensibility-wise.'

Familiarity is an important part of your projects. Since familiarity means something different to everyone, how does the concept work in practice?
PRIMO ORPILLA: During the workday, people have their rituals. What we do is to design spaces that they feel respond to them. If our research tells us that employees do their best work when they go to a café or to happy hour at the local pub, or that they enjoy meeting with clients in an apartment-style setting, we don't discount any of that information, because the more comfortable they are – that's what we mean when we say 'familiar' – the quicker they adapt to the environment. We use the term 'invisible workplace' to refer to a space that is so comfortable it just fades away, and you don't even realize that you are working. ↳

Studio O+A describes the fully
equipped meeting spaces at Uber 11
as 'freestanding mini-ecosystems'.

Nominated for The Great Indoors Award 2015 (see p. 195), Uber Office 11th Floor by Studio O+A has an unfinished look that reflects the 'work in progress' vibe so characteristic of a start-up.

Photos Jasper Sanidad

'When a workplace is *too sterile* or formal, people are less inclined to share ideas'

↰ **Workspaces have become far more democratic in recent times, and hierarchical boundaries have disappeared. But an increasingly open-plan office comes at the cost of private or personal space. How do you solve that problem?** The whole idea of open plan is that you can see everybody and see the work that is going on. But if you don't do open plan with additional ancillary spaces – such as living rooms, shelters and war rooms – then you won't have a functioning workplace. You will have a high-density workplace but one that doesn't account for multi-generational employees who are used to working with a little bit more enclosure, for instance. An open arrangement of workstations isn't enough; you need to provide other areas as well. For open plan to be collaborative, the office requires areas for quiet and socializing too.

Isn't the invisible workplace you've described somewhat risky? Shouldn't we be designing offices that encourage people to go home instead of tempting people to stay at work even longer? If the alternative is a sterile and uninviting work environment that is rife with hierarchy, then no. What we try to do is to make the experience more enjoyable and more relevant. The average American worker gets only ten days of paid vacation a year. People spend a lot of time at the office and are doing great work there – hopefully their life's work or something they believe in. In tech, especially, everybody believes they are changing the world. Why shouldn't that experience get better? In a lot of ways the new workspaces are less prescriptive than those of the past; you're free to come and go as you want.

Another way workplaces are changing is evident in the shrinking ratio of desks to people. What do you think about that? Nesting and having personal things around you while you work – that's not going to change, but we are finding that people are bypassing their desks and going straight to the couches to work on their laptops. Five years from now, Millennials will make up about 50 per cent of the workforce, and they keep things on their phones, iPads and laptops. For a lot of people, the workspace is in their backpack. I'm designing workstations [for furniture manufacturer Martin Brattrud] that have no desk. You can reconfigure the unit to make it a bit more enclosed, but it doesn't have a desk.

You design a lot for the tech sector. Do you get inspiration from other sectors too? Everybody is a tech company now; everybody has some sort of presence on the web. We try to make human-based design assumptions. People are methodical and ritualistic by nature, and behaviour is often shaped by our environment. So whether it's a bank, a creative ad agency or a hardcore tech company, we look at people and how they work best. We try to understand who is occupying the space and design for them. That is why we don't get the information we need only from a company's executives, who might not be connected to the people working on the floor.

Workplace design has gone from cubicles to open plan to offices that look almost like playgrounds. What's next? We are going to need variety. We also have to learn how to slow things down a bit – how to ↳

'For a lot of people, the workspace is in their *backpack*'

Primo Orpilla uses the term 'invisible workplace' to describe an environment that is 'so comfortable it just fades away, and you don't even realize that you're working'.

↰ create spaces in the workplace for recharging and regeneration, for something less digital and more analogue. We have a typology called the 'workshop'. The idea is that you go into a room where there's no technology, so you play a board game or a musical instrument, or you simply do something with your hands. Sometimes employers put machine shops or bike-repair shops in these areas. We know that if you are continually cranking code all day long, you're using only one part of your brain. We are seeing offices today without Wi-Fi or at least with areas that offer relief from digital devices. Workers need respite from our hyper information-driven world.

What about smart offices that monitor what you're doing, that can predict your behaviour and respond accordingly? Is this the office of the future? I'm sure you know that expression about how children should be seen and not heard. Well, technology should be that way too. I think it should be omnipresent, but without hindering you. We are working on next-generation meeting spaces that know what your last presentation was and pop it up on the screen, while adjusting the temperature of the room according to its location. But you should be able to unplug from smart options. An office that knows and reports where you are all the time is like Big Brother. You need an 'off' or 'kill' switch. People like to socialize, work at their own pace and surround themselves with things that remind them they're human. ✕

o-plus-a.com

WORK

For the office of Chinese e-commerce company Alibaba, Studio O+A combined classic elements with raw concrete and exposed ductwork.

Five steps to *future-proof* offices

Photo Jasper Sanidad

PREPARE FOR DEPARTURE
Commissioned by K9 Ventures, the designers at Cha:col gave the technology firm's Palo Alto warehouse – an incubator for start-ups – a bare-bones interior that encourages occupants to grow fast and move on.

Pressure Cooker

FROM FUN-FILLED TO STRIPPED-BACK: FORMULAS FOR THE CREATION OF PRODUCTIVE WORKPLACES FLIP 180 DEGREES.

SHUT OFF
Conceived by the architects at Slovenian firm Dekleva Gregori, (Un)curtain Office in Ljubljana features a flexible system of curtains that allows for communal areas as well as for private meeting rooms.

Photo Janez Marolt

'IT seems like comfort these days is vastly preferred over challenge.' These are the words of OMA director Rem Koolhaas, speaking about creativity at the Cannes Lions' Oglivy & Inspire lectures. 'The working environment now doesn't really look like an office any more – deliberately.' As he talks, a background presentation depicts informal office settings with staff in sneakers and jeans and walls covered in Post-its. 'Creativity and innovation seem more and more isolated as unique experiences that need a kind of hothouse atmosphere to even occur.'

Outside the lecture room, his words are illustrated by images of playground-like offices – a phenomenon whose epicentre is Silicon Valley – that offer employees everything from table-tennis equipment to pubs. With such an array of amenities, why leave your home – or should I say office – at all? True to the 'work hard, play hard' philosophy, workspaces like these make you content to stay where you are. But although they

are designed to facilitate creativity, is that really what they achieve? Employees might hang around 24/7, but how many of those hours are productive? 'Creativity should not depend on all the overgrowth of design and niceness that it has today,' says Koolhaas. And clearly he is not the only one in doubt about the effectiveness of sprawling workplaces, as an increasing number of architects advocate a more stripped-back approach to office design.

There are plenty of success stories that started in a student dorm or the neighbour's basement. Doesn't this suggest that reducing distractions to a bare minimum is a good way to raise productivity? K9 Ventures, a Palo Alto outfit that describes itself as 'a technology focused micro VC fund', believes just that. The company's goal is 'to bring seed-stage start-ups' out of the garage and into a place where they can be monitored and mentored. In keeping with that thought, K9 commissioned multidisciplinary firm Cha:col to design the interior

of its warehouse 'as close to bare bones as possible. Nobody should feel comfortable enough to stay too long.' Aptly titled The Kennel, the incubator space features a retrofitted shipping container with plywood wall covering. Just the idea of being surrounded by giants like Google, which occupies most of the surrounding buildings, should generate sufficient stimulation for the fledgling techies.

The architects at Slovenian firm Dekleva Gregori say that offices should respond to constant changes in a company's organization. (Un)curtain Office – their design for a workspace in Ljubljana – has no fixed partitions and can adapt to any situation. A system of natural-wool curtains allows for communal areas as well as for private meeting rooms.

Despite the generally accepted premise that energizing environments are the birthplace of revolutionary ideas, when stimulation becomes distraction, the need for concentration rises, along with the need for spaces that support intense focus. — **FK**

FRAME   In the digital magazine, Rem Koolhaas discusses challenge versus comfort in the workplace

SHOULDERS BACK
Posture, a tailor-made fashion collection by Jeffrey Heiligers, was designed to 'correct the poor postures of the digital generation'.

Health Kick

DOCTORS CONTINUALLY WARN US OF THE PERILS OF SITTING – ARE EMPLOYERS FINALLY GOING TO SIT UP AND LISTEN?

Photo Daantje Bons

WHEN you consider all its capabilities, it seems unlikely that the human body was created to sit in front of a screen all day, tapping away. Aches and pains in neck and shoulders after a long stint at the computer are testament to this. Recent studies point to a bit more than a niggling shoulder as a side effect, and research is suggesting even more shocking consequences. Martha Grogan, cardiologist at the Mayo Clinic, says: 'For people who sit most of the day, their risk of heart attack is about the same as smoking.' Others in the scientific community have started referring to the long-term effects of a sedentary life as the Sitting Disease.

It appears that some employers are starting to get the message. Rapt Studio, enlisted by Google to design its office in Irvine, California, has appealed to the competitive spirit of the search-engine's staff in a bid to stimulate activity by installing health-focused elements in Google's customary, fun-filled work environment. Sensors and LEDs embedded in a steel and perforated-acrylic staircase that winds its way up the four-storey building display stats based on its usage and the distances climbed by individuals.

Incorporating features that actively increase mobility is not unique to Google, however. Staff at Alphabeta in London's Finsbury Square – a complex refurbished and extended by Studio Rhe – may be more inclined to cycle to work now that the building sports a cycle ramp that allows users to go from street to desk with minimal effort.

While both Google and Alphabeta are clearly taking some tentative steps in the right direction, one wonders whether such attempts will be enough to meet the alarming concerns highlighted by the experts. The Well Living Lab at the Mayo Clinic in Minnesota is taking things decidedly further, conducting ↳

HAVE NO SEAT
Pulling workers away from their desks, OffSize by Léon de Lange for Prooff targets our natural urge to hang and lean.

'For people who sit most of the day, their risk of *heart attack* is about the same as smoking'

SERVE THE CYCLIST
Cycling commuters can ride directly into Alphabeta, a London complex that features a bike ramp.

Photo Hufton + Crow

Photo Eric Laignel

WATCH YOUR STEP
Wired with sensors and LEDs, the stairway
at Google's office in Irvine, California – a
workspace designed by Rapt Studio – tracks
the distances climbed by individual employees.

↰ tests that get to the core of how people work and how current work habits can damage their health. The lab investigates the 'real-world' impact on health and wellbeing in its one-of-a-kind facility. Armed with a reconfigurable environment, researchers can simulate a variety of workspaces and track every movement of their subjects with sensors and remote monitors.

Results coming from research labs indicate that giant strides will be made in future offices, but what happens in the meantime? If the repercussions affecting the health of sedentary workers are so drastic, surely we should be integrating immediate solutions into existing workspaces.

Prooff – a furniture brand established by Rianne Makkink and Jurgen Bey (see p. 050) – has been a source of products for the progressive office since its inception in 2006. A recent addition to the line is OffSize by Léon de Lange, whose irregular upholstered forms can be attached to walls or laid out on the floor to encourage impromptu chairless conversations.

Design Academy graduate Jeffrey Heiligers takes a similarly direct approach. His fashion collection, Posture, invites workers themselves to take more control of the situation. Heiligers' garments have seams sewn in areas that make stooping and slouching uncomfortable, thus forcing the wearer to sit up straight. The more the clothes are worn, the less they are needed.

One thing is for sure. Employers ought to take the wellbeing of their employees seriously. Business owners who make a deliberate move towards a healthier work environment not only reap the benefits of a happier workforce; they can also count on a more productive output. — **EM**

GO GREEN

Channelling the Health Kick trend, plant-filled offices make work feel like a walk in the park.

Staff at Ampersand's London office can brew their own tea from plants growing in the balustrade of the building's 12.5-m-tall Living Staircase, the work of Paul Cocksedge Studio and Arup.

Photo Mark Cocksedge

'We spend 90 per cent of our time indoors and 90 per cent of the cost of a building are the occupants, yet indoor environmental quality and its impact on health and productivity are often an afterthought,' says Joseph Allen, lead author of a recent study on the link between sustainable green office environments and cognitive function, conducted by the Harvard T.H. Chan School of Public Health's Center for Health and the Global Environment, SUNY Upstate Medical University, and Syracuse University. One outcome: air quality has a profound effect on the performance of workers.

Studies like this do not go unnoticed. A growing number of employers provide their staffs quite literally with a breath of fresh air. As aptly noted by popular columnist ↳

Schemata Architects turned the top floor of a former factory in Sumida, Tokyo – now housing the private office of Japanese kimono artist Hiroko Takahashi – into a green oasis.

Photo Shiori Kawamoto

↰ Ronald Hooft in *Frame* 107 (p. 077), plants are in. While the inclusion of a token plant wall or a couple of hanging baskets is a nod towards an eco-friendly workplace, some office interiors take *au naturel* to another level. In Seattle, Amazon's Biosphere Headquarters has begun to take shape. Due to open in 2017, the online heavyweight's new urban campus will consist of three gigantean greenhouse-like domes that will house, according to the rumour mills, young and mature trees. Biosphere's architects – a team from NBBJ, which has offices worldwide – want to give staff the fresh-air feel of being in a park, as well as to encourage interaction and collaboration. — **EM**

Photos Terje Ugandi

Architects Jan Skolimowski and Maie Raud of Kamp Arhitektid placed 5-m-tall trees – made of real tree trunks to which they added artificial branches and leaves – inside an office for Lenne, an Estonian manufacturer of children's clothing.

Photo José Hevia

MAKE NO DISTINCTION
Separated by no more than a transparent glass wall, staff and executives share a table at the Relojería Alemana office in Palma de Mallorca, Spain. The interior was designed by Ohlab.

Common Room

TRANSPARENT WORKSPACE INTERIORS CHALLENGE TRADITIONAL OFFICE HIERARCHY.

DON'T HIDE
At tech company Xiaomi's São Paulo location – with office interiors by local firm Arkiz – lounge areas leave employees undisturbed but not unseen.

Photo Studio Thiago Henrique

MENTION cubicles and what comes to mind are terms like 'battery hens' and 'corporate zombies' – certainly nothing remotely related to 'stimulation'. But reading about the original intentions behind Action Office, a system that Herman Miller launched in 1968, you find that enclosed workstations – the original cubicles – were seen as a revelation when presented as the world's first solution for open-plan offices. As president of the Herman Miller Research Corporation, Robert Propst analysed the way people worked in order to design flexible structures that could be combined in all sorts of ways. Clearly he wasn't thinking of the kind of static arrangement his cubicles ended up being known for, but it's *this* identity that has triggered a more casual approach to workspace design. Just imagine: around 2,800 employees will share a room at the new Frank Gehry-designed Facebook campus in California, which has the largest open-floor plan in the world.

Although the open-plan office is winning terrain (again), the concept is also the victim of increasing criticism. Propst's assumption that employees occasionally need privacy has made its way into the 21st century, a move that doesn't imply the adoption of an anonymous office culture. 'We can design offices that tap into a simple fact of human nature: people tend to share information more freely with those they know

BREAK DOWN BORDERS
With the use of glazed partitions in the Shanghai office occupied by Leo, the designers at LLLab challenged 'the controversial term "transparency" as applied to the stereotypic Chinese working hierarchy'.

personally than with those who are simply colleagues. Easy interaction enables more than just knowledge exchange; it creates a humane environment that attracts people and makes them feel valued. It provides the warmth and normality that is often missing from the functional workplaces that we've had for years,' says Steve Gale of M Moser Associates. You can have a reintroduction of partitions and still maintain an air of transparency. Meetings behind closed doors are passé, while open communication is promoted.

Designed by LLLab, the Shanghai office of digital agency Leo is notable for its glass-partitioned offices and meeting spaces. Apart from being very functional – daylight penetrates to the very heart of the space – glazing was intended 'to challenge the controversial term "transparency" as applied to the stereotypic Chinese working hierarchy'. Ohlab dismantles the classic order as well. A 14-m-long table is at the centre of the office that the studio designed for jewellery retailer Relojería Alemana in Palma de Mallorca, Spain. Both staff and executives use the table as a desk. Nothing but a glass wall separates the boardroom from the main workspace.

Another tendency within today's work sphere sees CEOs from the likes of Indiegogo and Meetup exchanging the coveted corner office for, well, no office at all. They want to demonstrate their accessibility and improve communication within their organizations. Developments such as this signal a shift towards a more democratic office with a less dominant pecking order. — FK

Photo Peter Dixie

PUT IT TO THE TEST
By conducting an experiment that slowly turned a flexible workspace into a rigidly uniform environment, Studio Knol criticized current views on office design.

Brand Bait

**THE OFFICE
ENVIRONMENT
IS EMPLOYED
AS A TOOL FOR
RECRUITMENT
AND BRANDING.**

 The digital magazine offers the full breadth of King's Stockholm office

FOR most of us, the days of working solely for a paycheque are long gone. Employees are looking for satisfaction in their jobs and for bosses who care what happens to them. As a result, companies are adapting workspaces to the requirements of the staff, in hopes of attracting and retaining a good workforce.

Set to hit our screens this year, the film adaptation of Dave Eggers' novel, *The Circle*, features a young girl who is hired by an influential internet company. The campus of this futuristic tech business offers everything an employee can imagine, and Mae Holland is wowed by the impressive amenities. Along with its forward-looking reputation, the company lures the smartest minds with sensational perks.

Off-screen something similar is happening: the act of recruitment is being reconsidered. Finding your dream job should be like finding your dream partner, according to Elevated Careers, a service on the brink of being inaugurated by dating site EHarmony. With years of experience in helping people to find love online, EHarmony is poised to continue matchmaking on a more professional level by assisting people whose aim is a perfect position with an ideal company.

Commissioned by MU, an art venue in Eindhoven, Studio Knol proved the importance of an attractive workplace with a cheeky socio-architectural experiment for Dutch Design Week. Co-working space Out of Office, designed to serve the city's 21st-century flex workers, was equipped with ↳

Designed as an embodiment of the brand that occupies the premises, the office is becoming the *new showroom*

REFLECT YOUR PRODUCT RANGE
In Stockholm, Adolfsson & Partners transformed the office of game developer King into a series of whimsical landscapes that lead visitors through an amusement park based on gaming scenery.

Photo Adrien Williams

TAKE CENTRE STAGE
True to the spirit of an outfit that turns parties into immersive experiences with its wearable LED technology is PixMob's new Montreal headquarters, a club-slash-workshop-slash-office designed by Jean de Lessard.

↰ swings and an office rabbit. Slowly but surely, as the office became more strictly disciplined and dismal, its users – a group of trendy, highly perceptive freelancers – displayed the anticipated 'flight behaviour'.

On the 28th floor of a Manhattan skyscraper, IA Interior Architects created a clubby interior for a sales team working for a well-known social networking site for professionals. Besides a fitness room and informal lounges, the 'office' includes a hidden speakeasy that can be entered only by those who know which of the 133 vintage rotary phones mounted on the wall outside allows access to the room.

Apart from attracting employees with excessive facilities, companies also entertain clients

with expressive spaces. Visiting the Stockholm office of game developer King is like being transported into the animated world of games. Designed by Adolfsson & Partners, the Kingdom reflects the virtual, fairy-tale landscapes that appear in the company's main product.

Designed as an embodiment of the brand that occupies the premises, the office is becoming the new showroom – a clear manifestation of a company's corporate identity. — **FK**

Photo Eric Laignel

FOR MEMBERS ONLY
At a tech company's New York office, designed by IA Interior Architects, only members of the inner circle know how to access the hidden speakeasy by using the correct rotary phone.

TECH TALKS

Tecno CEO Giuliano Mosconi lists five ways in which smart office furniture is redefining the way we work.

1 Get personal

Interactive office furnishings place the individual at the centre of the workplace, connecting users to their environment and the objects that surround them. With io.T (Intelligence of Tecno, borrowed from the abbreviation for 'Internet of Things'), for example, users can customize and predefine workstation preferences to best suit their needs. As you approach Tecno's 'smart table', a built-in sensor recognizes your ID badge or phone and adjusts both room temperature and lighting to your liking, creating a personalized, interactive office environment.

2 Sharing is caring

The desire for smart products has never been greater. Objects alone cannot satisfy the growing demands of today's digitally connected world, however. We need objects that can perform more tasks. Tecno's custom-designed io.T cloud allows you to safely store and send information without the hassle of external devices.

3 Think outside the cubicle

Flexibility and freedom are redefining the future of the workplace. Intelligent interactive office furnishings provide both. With io.T, you can not only share and send material; you can also

I am setting the temperature as you have requested between 21 24 °C

Together with Turin-based design collective GTP, Tecno introduces io.T, an interactive workstation that fuses office furniture and computer technology.

Photo Germano Borrelli

work at any desk or location. Is your regular table already taken? No problem. The io.T app tells you which tables are available nearby.

4 Work towards a healthier planet

A lot of earth's energy supply is wasted on office spaces that are vacant or not occupied full time. It's not enough to know how many people are in a building. It's also important to know where they are and what they are doing. Io.T interacts with a building, keeping track of requirements and performance levels, and monitoring internal and external factors like climate, traffic and energy consumption.

5 See things from an *object*-ive perspective

Connectivity today goes beyond human communication to include object-to-human and object-to-environment interconnectedness. Io.T's interaction with both user and environment encompasses everything from security and ID checks to energy and maintenance controls. By merging physical and digital realms, Tecno's latest innovation adds a new dimension to the workplace, one that is more personal, more efficient and more cost-effective. In one word: comprehensive. — MO

INCITE COMMUNICATION

Vitra developed the Studio Office in collaboration with architect Sevil Peach. The open-plan space, which can be viewed at Vitra's headquarters in Birsfelden, Switzerland, is composed of five neighbouring clusters that stimulate interaction.

Photo Ariel Huber, courtesy of Vitra

Nomadic Notion

FIND OUT WHO CATERS FOR THE FLOW OF GLOBETROTTERS NOW COMBINING BUSINESS, TRAVEL AND LEISURE.

KEEP IT CLASSY
Catering for people looking for a bit more luxury in a shared workplace, The Office Space commissioned Woods Bagot to fit out Sydney's Art Deco Paramount House, where sophisticated office suites are clad in American cherry.

GET COMMUNAL
WeWork Metropool, a new shared workspace in Amsterdam, demonstrates the American company's continued support of freelancers worldwide.

T H E world is becoming well accustomed to the idea that work doesn't always take place between four walls in the hours from nine to five. Business traverses boundaries of space and time. Deals are struck in hotel lobbies. Proposals are composed on intercity trains and contracts signed in airport lounges. As a result, business has become even more ingrained in the hospitality industry. Buzzwords – a marketplace for them if there ever was one – such as *bleisure*, *jobbatical* and the near unforgivable *bizcation* – are becoming commonplace. The jobbatical gained prominence soon after Estonian entrepreneur Karoli Hindriks launched a website of that name in 2014, which hooks up employers with talented job-seekers worldwide who are interested in combining globetrotting with short-term work opportunities.

Of course, the hospitality industry is quickly cottoning on to the burgeoning market. Airbnb jumped on the bandwagon with the addition of a feature that makes it easy for business people to keep track of expenses, select homes suitable for business travel or even find accommodation for a whole team. This initiative and others like it are streamlining today's global hot-desking.

In Amsterdam, Zoku – the self-proclaimed 'end of the hotel room as we know it' – is building a reputation by meeting the demands of a new type of business clientele. Targeting global nomads who want more than a place to rest their weary heads, Zoku offers co-working spaces that extend beyond quiet areas of the lobby. Designed in collaboration with Concrete, the bedrooms are more ↳

Business has become even more ingrained in the *hospitality industry*

↰like live/work studios, which can be rented for a few nights or for a couple of months if desired. Instead of a bed – which is tucked away out of sight – a large kitchen table is the focal point of each unit. In contrast with more traditional hotels, which don't encourage a guest to have friends or colleagues drop by, Zoku invites clients to use their rooms for anything from dinner parties to brainstorming sessions.

Design Academy Eindhoven graduate Shay Raviv addresses the link between business and hospitality with Hôtel Travail. Her practical proposal for merging professional online networks and existing hospitality locations comprises a number of 'stations' that facilitate the diverse requirements of today's workers. Elements such as Wi-Fi Shelters and Debate Carousels are nifty examples of how hospitality might profit from the growing market through the integration of imaginative extras and novel additions.

Even if designers and architects continue to address the needs of the restless desk-hopper, the final destination is not the only aspect that deserves attention. Trains, planes and their respective waiting areas have a long way to go before reaching the level of detail already achieved in accommodation. Top-tier travellers are currently reaping the benefits of certain ideas sketched here – consider Ilse Crawford's recent intervention at Hong Kong International Airport's new Pier First Class Lounge – but surely communal areas that are accessible to economy-class passengers have business potential too. Ticket for one to a quiet workspace en route? Yes, please. — **EM**

FOSTER VERSATILITY
In Madrid, Jump Studios took charge of Google's sixth co-working campus, where formal and informal spaces provide room for pre-accelerator programmes, business mentoring and more.

Photo Gareth Gardner

HYBRID HOT-HOUSE

The interior of Second Home's headquarters invites nature to enter the building. The plan is to grow full-size trees between the new floors.

Photo Iwan Baan

Serendipitous collisions should be the norm in today's workspaces, say Rohan Silva and Sam Aldenton, founders of London's collaborative workspace Second Home.

What led to the founding of Second Home? And of all the things to disrupt, why choose the workplace? ROHAN SILVA: With over half the world's population now living in urban areas, this is the most important time to be thinking about the future of the city. That's what Second Home is about – how to make our cities more livable, more sustainable, healthier – and how to achieve a built environment that might better support creativity and entrepreneurship. The workplace was the obvious starting point, as structural changes in the economy simply aren't adequately reflected in office design, and the likes of Regus and WeWork are obviously such soulless and cynical places.

Concepts of work and career have changed dramatically in the digital age. People are always on, and the divide between work and play is dissolving. How does Second Home respond to the end of the nine-to-five? RS: Second Home is open 24/7, so you can stay up late to hit that milestone if you need to. But that doesn't mean we're encouraging people to work all the time. There's a strong emphasis on wellbeing and on enabling people to interact and build relationships with one another.

Second Home has set itself apart through its complex ecosystem of businesses, rather than through the more familiar monocultural clumpings of tech versus design versus fashion et cetera. Why is that? RS: We believe that good things happen when different industries, ideas and people collide, which is why we work so hard to curate a broad range of companies – from fashion and design to technology and the arts. It's also why we place such an emphasis on events and architecture, to ensure that we create an environment where serendipitous collisions are the norm.

Second Home quickly became known for its sense of design and for your collaboration with SelgasCano, the Spanish firm that designed your London offices. Can you tell us more about the vertical extension? SAM ALDENTON: The reason we originally wanted to work with SelgasCano is their thoughtful approach to architecture, which supports creativity, innovation and wellbeing. Many of their spaces echo nature in a very beautiful way. Right now we're growing vertically, to occupy three additional floors upstairs. The extension will be incredible, with full-size trees between floors – growing under low-energy full-spectrum LED lights. Over 1,000 plants and trees will line the corridors. These living organisms will be fed by an advanced soil-free hydroponic irrigation system, which makes life a hell of a lot easier for the gardener. — JO
secondhome.io

Photo Pal Hansen

Rohan Silva (former senior policy adviser to Prime Minister David Cameron and the man behind the government's Tech City initiative) and Sam Aldenton (cofounder of Feast food festival and founder of the Dalston Roof Park) opened Second Home in 2014.

Out Now

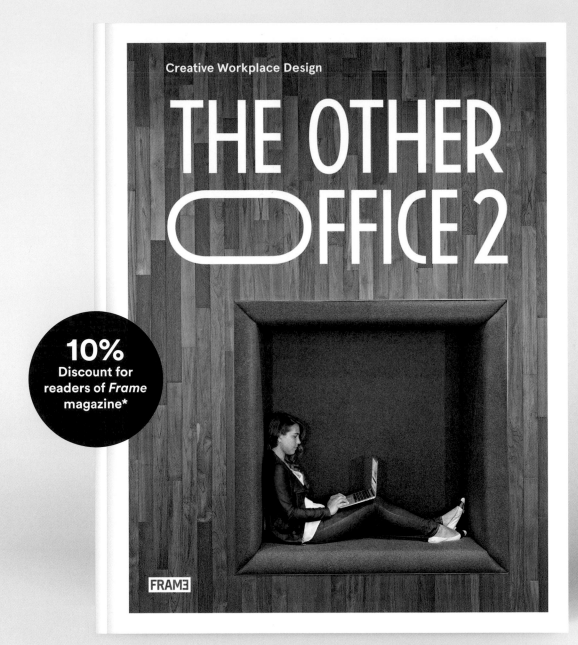

Inside Job

The leading trends in floors, walls and bathrooms

Livable and customizable bathrooms, breathable walls, and supersized ceramic tiles: interior products are <u>smarter</u> and more <u>sustainable</u> than ever. In this issue's special IMM LivingInteriors Report, we cover top trends in <u>sanitaryware</u>, <u>flooring</u> and <u>wallcoverings</u>.

Handmade in Portugal by local artisans, JoV's custom carpets merge traditional values with contemporary design.

Covering Ground

From mossy murals to customizable carpets, exhibitors at IMM's LivingInteriors embrace the leading trends in flooring and wallcoverings.

WORDS *Jane Szita*

Florim Ceramiche's patterned stoneware is available in nine extra-large formats: Magnum Oversize is a range of high-tech porcelain slabs for both commercial and residential projects.

Aleksandra Gaca's collaboration with Casalis resulted in the company's decorative 3D Architextiles, which feel both soft and tough. The intriguing wallcoverings provide good acoustic isolation.

1

Anything, Anywhere

Flexibility is key to floor and wall solutions of the future.

'**FUTURE** surface materials will combine many characteristics,' says Francis Vercaemst of Casalis. 'They will have to be flame-retardant, easy to clean, strong and sustainable. High acoustic performance, easy mounting and, of course, flexibility are all attributes that will define the next generation of materials.' Wall and floor finishes must increasingly be all things to all people – which is not a problem for Casalis's own Architextiles. These 3D woven fabrics have built-in versatility thanks to their familiar knit-look herringbone motif and neutral palette. They can be used in a wide variety of ways, for everything from beanbags to soundproofing panels.

Scalability is also a feature of Florim's Ceramiche Magnum Oversize slabs: porcelain stoneware tiles that are larger (up to 1.6 x 3.2 m) than any comparable product. All Florim brands – Floor Gres, Rex, Casa Dolce Casa and Casamood – include the jumbo slabs. With a thickness of just 6 mm, they are easy to cut to any shape or size for use on walls and floors, as well as doors, tables, kitchen counters, fireplaces and even furniture. 'The extreme practicality of this product, together with the wide range of surfaces on offer, means that we see it being used in highly flexible and personalized ways,' says Florim's Silvia Alonzo.

The oldest flexible floor covering is the carpet, and JoV is keeping up the tradition with its collection of customizable rugs: hand-tufted, hand-woven, hand-knotted or hand-knitted, they come in wool, silk, linen, mohair and cotton. Customers choose the size, shape, technique, material and colour of their rug, which is then handmade by Portuguese artisans. JoV states that one square metre of each rug takes four to five hours to complete, while assuring us that 'timing and delivery' are flexible. According to JoV: 'A luxury rug is not just decoration but a testimony to taste and character that expresses who you are.' ✕

Design Academy Eindhoven graduate Sam Linders' flexible Wobble-Up tiles function as both flooring and furniture.

2

Inspired by Nature

Surfaces increasingly reflect our need for nature.

'**A S** technology becomes more significant in our lives and interiors, nature is brought into the mix as a healthy counterpart,' says Nina Freund, CEO of Freund GmbH. 'In fact, it has never been more important to create the right balance.' Her company sets out to do this with moss walls and moss pictures, which are highlighted by real mosses and plants that give a green dimension to homes and offices. 'We make sure they are easy to install, and we give our customers extensive guidance,' she says. 'The mosses are cleaned and preserved using a special process. As a result, they maintain their natural green colour and do not need artificial light, special care or fertilizers.' In addition to their calming effect, the panels help regulate the indoor climate and absorb noise.

Moss is also the material used by Stylegreen for its Polemoss Ellipsoid, a circular 3D object featuring reindeer moss. The product, says CEO Niklas Guggenberger, brings 'nature to the home or office' at a time when many of us recognize a growing distance between our surroundings and the natural world. At IMM,

Stylegreen is also showing Flexmoss, a system that allows customers to build their own mossy walls. In addition to its exclusive use of naturally preserved materials and certified wooden frames, Guggenberger stresses that the company has 'shifted all production back to Germany' in an effort to raise its ethical profile.

Senses Working Overtime

Neolith's La Bohème sets out to capture the tactile essence of Lebanese cedar, with its bold grain and raw woody hue. Its special textured finish heightens the effect. Available in thicknesses of 6 or 12 mm, La Bohème is suitable for worktops, kitchen islands, wall cladding and flooring. 'Interior design concepts or products that are inspired by nature are predominant this year,' says TheSize's Mar Esteve Cortes. She points out that the Neolith range is natural not just in looks but also in essence: 'Neolith is 100 per cent natural and recyclable, as well as durable and extremely resistant to stains, heat, scratches, abrasion and wear, making it a very eco-friendly material.' ↳

The natural elements used in Freund's moss walls help regulate indoor climate without the hassle of plant maintenance.

Neolith's La Bohème takes it cue from the look of Lebanese cedar.

'As technology becomes more significant in our lives and interiors, nature is brought into the mix as a healthy counterpart'

NINA FREUND, FREUND

Printed on vinyl paper or EQ.Dekor coating, graphics for Inkiostro Bianco's Undressing Surfaces decorate walls, floors and ceilings.

↰ Visually, Inkiostro Bianco draws on many influences from the natural world for its new Undressing Surfaces wallcoverings, which seem to have peeled from the wall in layers, only to be re-layered to produce a unique effect with great subtlety and depth. Patterns and textures can be alternated to personalize the wall, and further options for the customization of graphics include two colour variations and three levels of decoration. The product can be applied to any surface (walls, floors, ceilings and furnishing accessories); graphics can be printed on vinyl paper or EQ.Dekor, a wallcovering made in collaboration with Mapei.

Sustainable Style

Carpeting for the catwalk is a collaborative project involving sustainable carpet company Ege and Danish fashion designer David Andersen. At IMM, their carpet couture collection showcases spectacular dresses made from Ege's Highline 1100 Ecoline, which uses recycled materials. 'Working with a textile such as carpet is immensely challenging,' says Andersen, who clearly relished the difficulty. 'By entering into this collaboration, we're not merely helping one another to move in a more sustainable direction; we're also helping to place greater focus on the area as a whole. It's unexpected and rather funny, yet we also have an important message that we'd like to send.'

Tecnografica's Natural wallpaper range combines impactful graphic design with strong sustainability. As the company's Stefano Lamberti explains: 'Our Natural wallpaper is 100 per cent eco-friendly, with absolutely no PVC and no chemical solvents in the inks, which are all water-based. All our wallpapers are accompanied by ecological and safety certification.' He notes that when it comes to wall and floor coverings, sustainability presents a challenge that concerns both business and ecology. 'Digital technology has boosted a lot of small and medium-sized companies, which can now make and print designs on various materials,' he says. 'In the future, all these companies will need the ability to endure and not burn out.' ✕

'Digital technology has boosted a lot of small and medium-sized companies'

STEFANO LAMBERTI, TECNOGRAFICA

Focused on sustainability, Ege's Highline 1100 Ecoline carpet uses recycled materials.

Kirsi Enkovaara displays the movement of water in a pattern-printing technique she calls Landscape of Gravity, which she applied to a series of tiles.

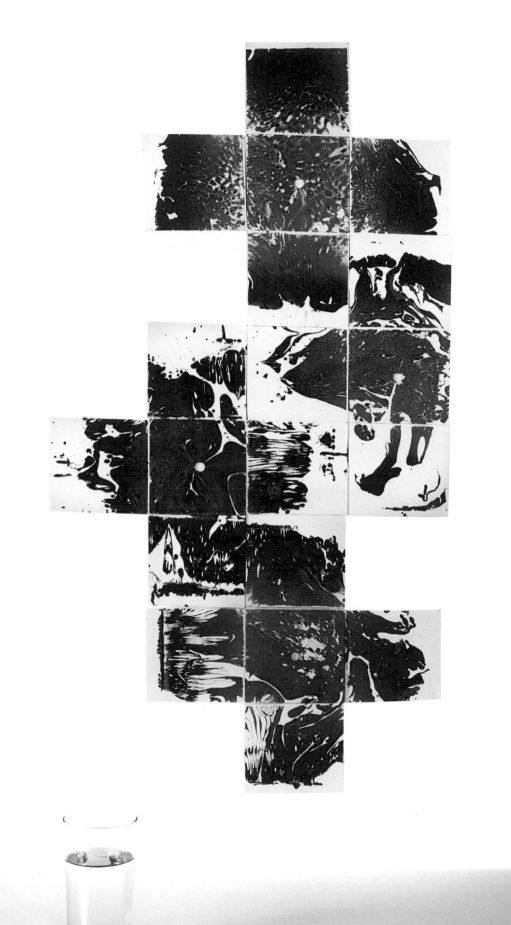

3

Smart Materials

Multifunctional and customizable surfaces lead the way to tomorrow.

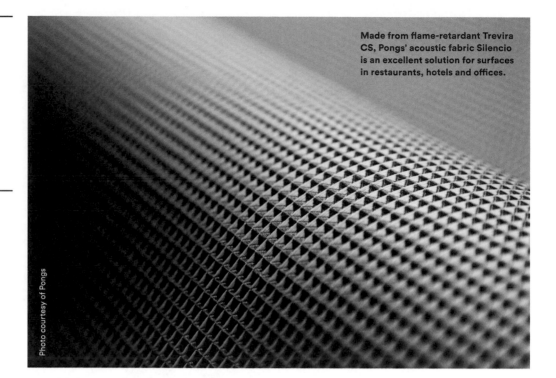

Made from flame-retardant Trevira CS, Pongs' acoustic fabric Silencio is an excellent solution for surfaces in restaurants, hotels and offices.

Photo courtesy of Pongs

'**BECAUSE** they are invisible, acoustics have been relatively neglected in architecture,' says Kenichi Sato, founder of Ply Project. As part of the company's mission to make plywood 'a smart engineered material for improving people's lives in the 21st century', Ply Project combines layers of plywood and foam to make Wavy, a lightweight, tactile material for acoustic applications. 'Simple cuts make the plywood sheet entirely flexible,' says Sato, who describes Wavy as panels with 'a flat, resilient surface that provides not only an aesthetic and organically natural appearance, but also acts as a reassessment of plywood'.

Pongs' Silencio is another innovative acoustic fabric that combines aesthetic and functional properties. In this case, Silencio owes its effectiveness to a distinctive 3D honeycomb structure. 'The three-dimensional surface refracts and absorbs sound waves, and has a positive effect on the perception of sound at the same time,' says Pongs' Michael Wartmann. 'In our opinion, the future of interior design will be determined by smart and flexible products like Silencio. To adapt to changing needs, products have to fulfil more than just one requirement. Aesthetics without practical function cannot fulfil contemporary demands.' He believes, however, that a well-functioning product ought to have an attractive design.

Imprilana shows how technology can make natural and traditional materials smart by updating them for a new generation of consumers. The company takes the most basic of materials, wool, and uses water-based dyes and the latest digital-printing technology to achieve a completely customizable result, which is possible, says the company's Thomas Klöbl, 'only with the use of digital systems. For more and more people, a perfectly matching interior is a must, and they are looking for flexible companies that can offer this. The market trend in interiors is for customized, personalized products.' ✕

'Products have to fulfil more than just one requirement to adapt to changing needs'

MICHAEL WARTMANN, PONGS

Ply Project's simple acoustic panel Wavy is effective thanks to simple cuts scored along a plywood sheet, which make the lightweight material flexible. Wavy panels are also suitable for furniture design.

Royal College of Art student Chao Chen envisions his humidity-responsive surfaces – based on a pine cone's reaction to water – as an architectural material that adapts to weather conditions.

GOING DIGITAL

Mosa's *Leandre la Fontaine* talks tiles and technology.

What inspired the Mosa Pattern Generator? We had many sources of inspiration, but what influenced us most were our close ties with architects. What we noticed from these relationships was a growing need for customization. The Mosa Pattern Generator is intended to give designers the freedom to develop different atmospheres, signatures and identities using our tiles. We wanted to break with traditional ideas that depict tiles as being purely functional.

How does your new software adapt to the user's circumstances or environment? The Mosa Pattern Generator is a user-friendly online design tool for making unique compositions with products from the entire Mosa range. As soon as a pattern is designed, it can be exported to 2D and 3D technical software programs such as AutoCAD and Revit, or 3D rendering tools such as Sketchup to create visualizations. In the future, users will be able to export their drawings to Bim-based programs as well.

How does the Mosa Pattern Generator reflect the needs of today's architects and designers? Today's designers are looking for greater flexibility. With the Mosa Pattern Generator, the possibilities are endless.

Mosa products can be combined in an infinite number of ways, which makes them an extremely versatile resource for architects and designers. Patterns can be as subtle or as vibrant as the designer likes. Surfaces are tailored to each project and are available in various styles, sizes and colours.

Advancements in technology have enabled Mosa to provide this service. **How do you see technology affecting the way you design products in the future?** Technology and online platforms will allow users to specify requirements and to be involved in every stage of the building process. Bim is a great tool in that regard, which is why we are looking to sync the Mosa Pattern Generator to this model-based software. ✕

mosa.nl/generator

With the Mosa Pattern Generator, designers who want a customized look can turn their ideas into visual imagery using Mosa's extensive library of products.

Surface to Air

Conceived in collaboration with *Frame*, i29's IMM LivingInteriors pavilion defies visitors' expectations.

CHARGED with designing a pavilion to house IMM LivingInteriors' collection of wall and floor coverings, Jasper Jansen and Jeroen Dellensen of i29 wanted to offer visitors a different take on the subject. 'Robert Thiemann of *Frame* magazine gave us three major trends to address,' Dellensen explains. 'These are "Inspired by nature", "Anything, anywhere" and "Smart materials". Within these three themes, we developed an overall concept that can be communicated in several ways.' Unity is provided by 'making one big gesture that is strong enough to display all the different trends in one'.

The pavilion plays with the idea of visibility and invisibility, using mirrored glass and lighting to generate a playful effect and to arouse visitors' curiosity. 'We wanted to play with optical illusion and space, and to trigger visitors to discover the different material installations in this pavilion step by step,' says Dellensen. 'Lately, the focus in our work at i29 is to create a sense of revelation and curiosity through spatial intervention. There is something intriguing about not being able to decipher the space you are entering at first glance.' In this pavilion, therefore, 'visitors are welcomed into an illusionary experience, where see-through mirrored surfaces give a glimpse of several installations spread out over the area'.

As guests arrive, they set off on a main pathway, which the designers refer to as 'trend avenue'. This then 'literally opens up into a square at the centre of the exhibition hall. We've placed several "experience boxes" in the square for the display of thematic scenes that refer to the three major trends. Inside these boxes, reflective walls produce a holographic effect that reveals the material's features. With light flashing on and off inside the boxes, the scenes seem to appear and disappear like a Fata Morgana.' Inside the volumes, a combination of light and sound adds to the immaterial feel of the reflected surfaces.

Immateriality as a design concept is an antidote to the overkill so often encountered at trade fairs, Dellensen believes. 'Trade fairs usually strike us as overcrowded places with an abundance of products,' he says. 'Most of the time, there is way too much of everything, so you don't experience the quality of the space and the products any more. By keeping it simple and being selective each time you make a choice, you can avoid the pitfalls.' ✕
i29.nl

SHOW STOPPERS

Frame's IMM LivingInteriors pavilion features fresh offerings from the industry's top brands, such as **Bauwerk Parkett, Casalis, Ege, Florim, Hi-Macs, Mosa** and **Neolith by TheSize**

The Me Space

Vola's Round-head shower can be wall- or ceiling-mounted. The shower has two flow options: 24 or 15 litres per minute.

Bathroom products on show at IMM's LivingInteriors announce a self-indulgent, wellness-centred approach to a space that was once purely functional.

WORDS *Jane Szita*

Scape Monolith, an elegant basin from NotOnlyWhite, is available with inlays of Bianco Carrara marble or Hi-Macs, a waterproof and visually seamless material.

'**THE** bathroom of the future will be a kind of private spa and wellness centre, where people spend significantly more time.' So says Peter Mechtold of Relax Your Life, whose Movy range shows IMM visitors exactly where the company thinks this trend is heading. Sinuous, stylish and waterproof, Movy furniture can be used in bathrooms, living rooms and even outdoors. 'Sitting, chilling and relaxing are activities that we will see increasingly in future wellness rooms,' says Mechtold. 'We expect fitness equipment and home entertainment to find their way into sanitary areas and to influence the type, use and design of interior products for those spaces.'

The growing focus on wellness means that more and more private residences boast the kinds of facilities familiar from an afternoon at the spa. Klafs' Sauna S1 is a perfect example of how improved construction methods and materials are enabling compact and flexible solutions for the home, without compromising on the desired experience. 'Our wood wall construction is 40 per cent lighter than the one used in a conventional sauna,' says Klafs' Rolf Glantz. 'S1 is designed as a completely self-contained mobile system. Your guest room, living room or workroom stays just the way it was before you installed the sauna – and you can take it with you when you move, just like a freestanding closet.'

Escape and Meditate

Vola CEO Gerald Cappek agrees that the modern bathroom has become 'an escape from worldly matters. A place to rejuvenate ↳

S1 from Klafs is the first sauna to retract into a 60-cm-deep recess – the depth of a standard bedroom closet – at the touch of a button.

Clay, quartz, feldspar and titanium oxide are the ingredients of TitanCeram, a material developed by Villeroy & Boch that highlights Artis, the company's premium washbasin collection.

> ## 'The modern bathroom is a place to rejuvenate the body, to allow the mind to empty and the soul to meditate'
>
> GERALD CAPPEK, VOLA

↰the body, to allow the mind to empty and the soul to meditate.' His company's new products – the Round Series hand shower and the Kneipp Hose and Waterfall Shower – reflect the shift in ambience. Their timeless design contributes to the sought-after sense of contemplation and, as Cappek points out, guarantees extended use and thus sustainability. 'The products all take their proportions from classic Arne Jacobsen taps designed more than 47 years ago,' he says. All come in polished or brushed chrome, in brushed stainless steel and in 14 colours.

Customization can be found in every niche of interior design, and the bathroom is no exception, says Marike Andeweg of NotOnlyWhite, whose latest range features Hi-Macs acrylic stone. The company's Scape collection comprises a series of simple elements, including wall-hung and freestanding basins and a freestanding unit, or 'monolith'. These pieces can be combined to make countless bathroom 'landscapes'

according to the user's preference. Three types of sink inlay – grid, blocks, or a single slab of Bianco Carrera marble – add to the options. 'It's about personalizing products and emphasizing the beauty of everyday things,' says Andeweg, whose glimpse into the future reveals the growth of 'made-to-measure solutions that add personality to surfaces through structure, colour and pattern'.

Creative Classics

Even the more classic sanitary products are undergoing a rethink. Artis, the new countertop washbasin series from Villeroy & Boch, revitalizes the ceramic sink by lending it an unusual air of lightness. Available in four traditional shapes – round, oval, rectangular and square – Artis owes its pared-down look to TitanCeram, a material developed by Villeroy & Boch. It's a combination of clay, quartz, feldspar and titanium oxide, says the company's Sandra Hettinger, explaining the collection's 'uniquely

precise forms with extremely thin walls and sharply drawn edges'. She also underscores the beneficial characteristics of ceramics, which are, in principle, 'completely natural and sustainable'.

For Geberit, today's accent on wellness is 'all about water', says the company's Grit Wehling, especially when it comes to the AquaClean Mera shower toilet. 'True, this type of toilet needs energy and more water than your ordinary WC, but the ecological rating of Geberit shower toilets is almost the same as that of traditional toilets, whose environmental impact includes an important factor: paper.' Wehling maintains that good design is becoming ever more important as the bathroom rises to the level of status symbol, citing a Zukunftsinstitut survey of 2013: 'It asked 1,000 people which is more important to them: new car, new music system or new bathroom. More than half opted for a new bathroom.' ✕

Axor One lets users control multiple water outlets with the back of the hand or the elbow.

GO WITH THE FLOW

What does Axor Hansgrohe's latest product say about the future of the bathroom? *Philippe Grohe* explains.

How does Axor One contribute to the brand's vision of the bathroom as a living space? Axor One allows a completely fresh interpretation of water control: by consolidating multiple individual controls into one simple element, it streamlines both the look and functionality of the bathroom. In other words, its all-in-one property declutters the shower space by incorporating all functionalities in one element. This opens up the traditionally confined bathroom, leaving ample room for an individual arrangement of the shower space, whether large or small.

Why was it important for Axor to develop a product with an all-in-one control system? We were aiming for something that would be intuitive, interactive and responsive without distracting from a soothing shower experience or cluttering the shower with unnecessary controls. The result is a system that activates and deactivates water flow by a mere tap on the 'paddles'. Clear symbols indicate specific water outlets: you can choose between overhead, hand or side shower. Temperature is set by turning a central dial, and a small lever directly below regulates water volume. It's possible to turn multiple water outlets on or off simultaneously, with the back of the hand or the elbow. All in all, Axor One provides a convenient and engaging shower experience.

What led you to collaborate with Barber & Osgerby on Axor One? It was a mix of our mutual admiration for each other's work and of meeting in the right place at the right time. Ed's and Jay's work in interaction design was perfect for what we wanted to create. We told them about the idea we had for the shower, and they convinced us that they were the right pair for the design of an object that would become Axor One.

Where do you predict the future of sanitary products is headed? From an aesthetic perspective, we will continue to see more materials and special finishes for bathroom fixtures. Our initiatives in this direction include crystal glass and porcelain spouts for Axor Starck V, as well as 15 standardized PVD finishes that range from red-gold to black chrome. In terms of functionality, the sanitary sector will continue to see investments in user comfort: easy-to-use products. Multifunctional modular systems, such as our Axor Universal Accessories collection, will support this idea by enabling users to customize their own bathrooms. ✗

hansgrohe-int.com

Geberit's WhirlSpray shower features two nozzles, uses a minimum of water, and provides a thorough yet gentle way to maintain personal hygiene.

Turn on your creativity
Mosa.

Forever Now

The jury of The Great Indoors Award 2015 honours radical and social approaches to interior design.

WORDS *Robert Thiemann*

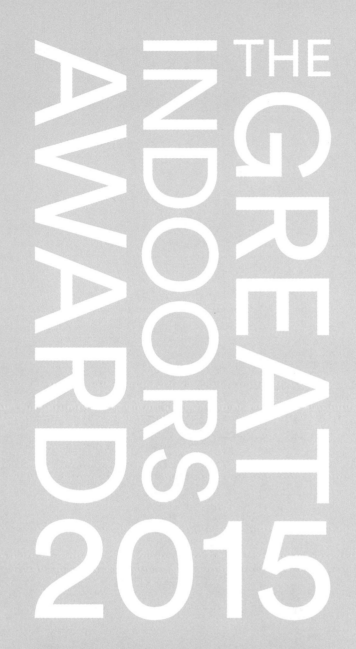

THE GREAT INDOORS AWARD 2015

WHEN a jury whose members have backgrounds as diverse as curation, education, manufacturing and interior design is asked to come to terms with 271 submissions to an interior-design competition, you might wonder about the criteria used to evaluate the various projects. The question becomes all the more relevant if the theme of the award is Forever Now, implying a focus on designs that define the present – projects emerging from an attitude that requires our attention to what is current, urgent and actual.

It's remarkable then how down to earth the answers are: from 'authentic spatial solutions that respond to location and the client's identity' to 'concepts of how we control spaces' and 'how communication, technology and materials deal with the contemporary'.

Voilà – a neat summary of views expressed by the jury of The Great Indoors Award 2015. But above all the jury was interested in ideas, because, in the words of Deyan Sudjic: 'If we're not judging ideas, then we're just judging appearances.'

In light of his statement, it will come as no surprise that the award-winners display a radical, often social approach to designing interiors. In RAAAF's ideas about future office life, chair and desk have made way for an activating workspace. India Mahdavi's pink colour scheme and inclusion of art work for London restaurant Sketch marvellously evokes

fin-de-siècle tea parlours, but with a distinctly modern twist. The ceramics store that Yusuke Seki designed in Nagasaki invites visitors to walk on what seems to be an installation of stacks of precious earthenware, which turn the showroom into an exciting visceral and acoustic experience. And what about the hotel that AllesWirdGut (German for 'all will be well') built in Vienna? It features 78 'designer rooms' for conventional guests and two apartments for refugees awaiting asylum. It puts the haves and the have-nots under one roof, facilitating an exchange between travellers who arrive by choice and those accommodated by necessity.

It's with concepts like these that designers and clients alike make headlines. They grab attention here and now, fulfilling one of the most important tasks of today's interior designer. But look a bit closer at this year's award-winners to discover an even deeper layer of intention, one that addresses the human condition. Isn't that something to keep in mind forever? ✕

THE GREAT INDOORS AWARD 2015
The jury of The Great Indoors Award 2015 consisted of Brendan Cormier (curator, Victoria and Albert Museum), Nora Fehlbaum (Co-CEO, Vitra), Alexis Georgacopoulos (director, ÉCAL), Jaspar Jansen (designer and cofounder, i29) and Deyan Sudjic (director, Design Museum). The jury assessed 271 submissions from 39 countries
the-great-indoors.com/2015

Concentrate & Collaborate

OFFICES, STUDIOS, ADMINISTRATION BUILDINGS, CONFERENCE CENTRES

Photo Jan Kempenaers

WINNER
THE GREAT INDOORS AWARD 2015

Photo courtesy of RAAAF

From left to right: Ronald Rietveld, Arna Mackic and Erik Rietveld of RAAAF put their seat-free ideas into practice.

The End of Sitting by RAAAF
Amsterdam

Although all submissions to the competition are thoughtful and well executed, not all of them push the boundaries and show us new ideas. This project is a prototype and a wonderfully creative attempt to think spatially about future workscapes. Formally reminiscent of Zaha Hadid's early paintings, the design is not about taste but about the subject being addressed. Will we, in 20 or 50 years, be working while leaning over, lying down or standing up?

r a a a f . n l

Photo Jasper Sanidad

Uber Office 11ᵗʰ Floor by Studio O+A
San Francisco

Uber represents a new breed of business in the service industry, and its offices express the essence of its innovative concept. This is the shape of *now* – a space that reflects the rhetoric of the casual; it encapsulates various atmospheres that facilitate informal gatherings, conveys today's fantasy about future office life, and sets a new norm for workplace design.

o-plus-a.com

Photo Dirk Weiblen

Photo Andrea Jemolo

Fendi Headquarters by Marco Costanzi Architects
Rome

The design brings life to the interior of fascist monument Palazzo della Civiltà Italiana, also known as Rome's Square Colosseum. This is in itself an achievement, since the building was designed originally as no more than a façade for showing off Mussolini's architectural ambitions. Both office and showroom fluently speak the high-end, glamorous language of the client.

marcocostanzi.com

Flamingo: The Attic by Neri&Hu
Shanghai

This well-designed, atmospheric workplace marks a layered attempt to open up the attic for professional use. With its dark colour scheme and rigorously disciplined lines, the office of consultancy firm Flamingo is a stagelike space imbued with a literary, neo-Victorian ambience.

en.neriandhu.com

Photo Alexander van Berge

Royal Auping by Ex Interiors
Deventer

Many of today's workplaces have been designed especially for office management; they facilitate the work of medium- to top-level managers and employees. In this building, the designers make an effort to accommodate factory workers as well. The unusual and well-executed scheme is based on a combination of natural materials and clear perspectives.

ex-interiors.nl

Relax & Consume

HOTELS, BARS, CLUBS, RESTAURANTS, SPAS, WELLNESS CENTRES

Photo Thomas Humery

WINNER
THE GREAT INDOORS AWARD 2015

Photo Christophe Berlet

Designer India Mahdavi reimagined the interior of Sketch, which includes over 230 drawings by David Shrigley.

The Gallery at Sketch Restaurant by India Mahdavi
London

A pink room with chairs and tables that look like lavishly decorated cupcakes or a *fin-de-siècle* tearoom? This place is all about being different. It's a total environment that challenges preconceptions by appealing to our senses in a dramatic way. Apart from its adventurous colour choice, the space is dotted with intriguing details and amusing framed illustrations by David Shrigley.

india-mahdavi.com

Hueso Restaurant by Cadena + Asociados Concept Design
Guadalajara, Jalisco

There's lots of strange stuff going on in this *cabinet de curiosités*. Dipped in a powdery white coating, the interior is a pastiche of bones designed to evoke Mexico's surrealist tradition and macabre All Souls' Day. It's a dreamy place – and is conjuring dreams not a major goal of any good restaurant?

cadena-asociados.com

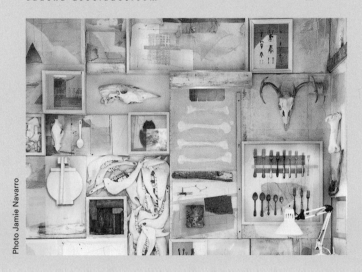

Photo Jamie Navarro

Photo Ali Bekman

Dardenia Restaurant by Alataş Architecture & Consulting
Istanbul

The restaurant offers a rare aesthetic combination of production and consumption. Thanks to a transparent floor in the dining area, guests have a theatrical view of the kitchen. The light, airy interior is enhanced by the use of striking contrasts.

ahmetalatas.com

Sala de Despiece Restaurant by Ohlab
Madrid

With one grand gesture, Ohlab makes the most of a tiny space in Madrid: a white cutting board that runs through the entire interior allows for preparing, cooking and eating food. The metaphor and its materialization are consistent with the fish dishes on the menu. An intelligent, effective use of material and space.

ohlab.net

Photo Miguel de Guzmán

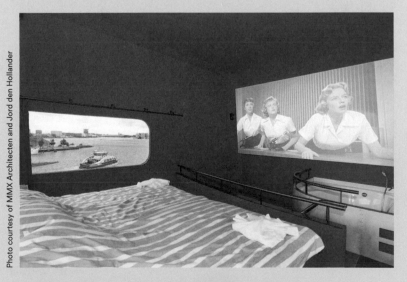

Photo courtesy of MMX Architecten and Jord den Hollander

Loft Letters: Botel by MMX Architecten with Jord den Hollander
Amsterdam

A very smart spatial design that envelops pop culture and draws hordes of visitors, Loft Letters converts what might have been unsightly signage atop a boat into a brilliant marketing device. The makers see their work as a Robert Venturi 'Duck': a novel composition of compact hotel rooms with views of the Amsterdam IJ.

mmx-architecten.nl

Show & Sell

SHOPS, SHOWROOMS, TRADE-FAIR STANDS, EXHIBITIONS

Photo Takumi Ota

WINNER
THE GREAT INDOORS AWARD 2015

Photo Yosuke Owashi

Although only 37 years old, Yusuke Seki made history the main theme of the renovation project.

Maruhiro Flagship Store by Yusuke Seki
Nagasaki

To show and sell earthenware in a store with a floor of cast-concrete bowls is not only a functional mode of advertisement – the shop's open façade reveals a stunning installation of the products – but also a dilemma for visitors, who wonder whether they can walk on the surface. Taking the risk, many seize the opportunity to make selfies. This layered approach to retail design is worthy of further consideration.

yusukeseki.com

HIC Whitestore by XML
Amsterdam

Visitors to Amsterdam's red-light district now have a pristine shop that stocks hangover medicine. A design reminiscent of contemporary art installations, Whitestore shows how retail outlets might function in the future. The design rigour that went into this project makes a strong substantive statement.

x-m-l.org

Photo courtesy of XML

Photo Kozo Takayama

Band of Outsiders Flagship Store by Lot-Ek
Tokyo

The designers' installation features rotating display elements that are as eye-catching as they are functional. Referencing the interior of a clock, the flagship hints at the seasonal rhythm so familiar in fashion. Modular display units provide a flexible solution with a distinctive twist that is both nostalgic and futuristic.

lot-ek.com

Design Republic Design Commune by Neri&Hu
Shanghai

Preservation is a topic seldom explored by the makers of Shanghai's rapidly changing built environment. The architects and developers of this project brave the desire for newness without taking a historicizing approach. The space, with its great vistas and sightlines, serves a retailer that needs a spatially refined backdrop for its high-end interior products.

en.neriandhu.com

Photo Pedro Pegenaute

Photo Josefina Eikenaar (commissioned by Textile Museum)

Huisraad (Dutch for 'household goods') Exhibition by Studio Makkink & Bey
Tilburg

It is not easy to display textile in an experiential manner within a gallery context. In an effort to immerse visitors in an elegant and interesting scenographic setting, the designers craft a space that is light, elegant and filled with visual references.

studiomakkinkbey.nl

Serve & Facilitate

LIBRARIES, HOSPITALS, THEATRES, SCHOOLS

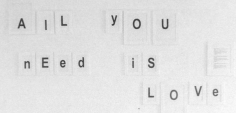

Photo Guilherme Silva Da Rosa

WINNER
THE GREAT INDOORS AWARD 2015

Photo Hertha Hurnaus

From left to right: Andreas Marth, Herwig Spiegl, Friedrich Passler and Christian Waldner founded AllesWirdGut in 1999.

Magdas Hotel by AllesWirdGut
Vienna

A project that deals with a notably topical and urgent social situation, Magdas is a hotel that welcomes conventional guests and refugees in the same manner, making no distinction between their financial circumstances and/or nationalities. A mix of second-hand furniture, natural materials and soft tones, the hotel has a homey feel. Of all the competition entries, it has the most visible social purpose, enabling encounters among users with the help of design.

alleswirdgut.cc

Photo Toshiyuki Nishimatsu

Kawaii Preparatory School by Matsuya Art Works / KTX ArchiLAB
Kobe

The architects' display for a school on a busy street opens up and 'advertises' the building. Bright colours and geometric forms appeal to a target audience of young girls. In a highly competitive environment with lots of schools, such a display seems to be an effective way to attract pupils. It can be seen as a shop window with a functional programme that includes spaces for formal meetings, classroom activities and casual get-togethers.

matsuya-art-works.co.jp
ktx.space

Photo Laura Torres Roa

Kaleidoscope: Space for Children by A2 Arquitectos
Mallorca

A series of playful objects turns a former squash court into a playground for kids. Variables such as external elements, natural light and youngsters on the move generate a range of shadows and reflections, modifying the space and producing multiple worlds that invite children to enter. A performative and visually gratifying design.

a2arquitectos.com

Public Library by Ministerie van Verbeelding
Schiedam

Housed in an old marketplace, Schiedam's public library aims to redefine the ways in which knowledge, literature and culture are made accessible and available to a wide audience. A composite of functions, the design plays with the building's 19th-century listed architecture. Among other moments of surprise and wonder, users discover a lush green courtyard.

ministerievanverbeelding.nl

Photo Piet Pulles

Photo Junten Morita

Shed of Leaf: Memorial and Space for Contemplation by G Architects Studio
Ibaraki

With simple means, an existing structure is transformed into a place that prompts visitors to contemplate the tsunami of 2011. The ephemeral gesture combines a simple interior with elements such as wind, reminding us of the force of nature and renewing awareness of the constant state of flux that influences every facet of our lives.

g-archi.info

Designed in Norway, Made in Holland

Febrik teams up with Nordic designers Anderssen & Voll to give rise to Drop, a series of textile 'skins' that interlace colour with form.

WORDS *Will Georgi*

M O S T people associate Febrik with lush, voluminously woolly textiles. It's an image that Renee Merckx, the brand's creative director, is proud of, as it's these 'fierce' materials that established Febrik as the manufacturer of the most innovative woollen products on the market. After a few years of enjoying the prestige involved, however, she wanted to try something new: something smaller. For the latest collection, Merckx called on Anderssen & Voll, aka Torbjørn Anderssen and Espen Voll. You might recognize them as the designers of Tibu, a swivel bar stool for Magis; Oslo, their sofa for Muuto; or the indoor gardening project they developed for Mjölk.

The Norwegian duo's background may be furniture, but their versatility has led to designs – now in the making – as diverse as cast-iron wood-burning stoves; objects for preparing, brewing and drinking coffee in the mountains of East India; and cast-iron art pieces to be introduced as their own brand.

High on the list of Febrik's priority projects is Eva, a chair for LK Hjelle, and Soft Grid, a collection of cushions for Muuto: both represent the joint efforts of Merckx and Anderssen & Voll. The partnership that evolved prompted Merckx to continue the collaboration, in order to add a Norwegian sense of balance to Febrik's product range. 'When Torbjørn and Espen visited us about

three years ago, they brought two little embroidered samples. I think they made them on the plane. They were really cute, and we tried to capture the same structure and feeling in Drop – not really a pattern, but something more skinlike.'

Funnily enough, Voll picks up the thread in our conversation a few days later. 'We've done a lot of sofas over the years, so it made sense to focus on the skin of the sofa in parallel. All our textile work can be seen as the outer layer of a three-dimensional object. For this reason, we often use micro-reliefs, textures that change character and reveal details when viewed from different angles or from different distances. The

DROP

Number of prototypes 12 **Colourways** 29
Composition 60% wool, 20% polyester,
20% polyamide **Application** Upholstery
covering **Martindale abrasion test** 60,000
cycles **Sustainability certification** Complies
with REACH legislation and OEKO-TEX 100
Inventory Stocked **Weight** 600 gr/m²

**Textile brand Febrik got together with
Anderssen & Voll to develop Drop,
a two-tone fabric that blends Nordic
design with Dutch workmanship.**

technique triggers a dialogue between
object and textile.'

Much to Merckx's delight, the
process went smoothly. 'It can take a couple
of years to transform an idea into the right
design and fabric, but Drop went really
fast. Torbjørn and Espen know exactly how
everything works here, so we could skip the
guide to knitting and crack on straight away.'

It quickly emerged that Drop would
be a two-tone fabric of the kind described by
Voll: the perception of colour changes under
the influence of light and viewing angle. The
only sticking point was the palette itself. 'We
had a lot of fun throwing pink next to green
and purple,' Merckx recalls. 'The material

looked just like a caterpillar. We wanted to fill
the product line with lots of kinky colours, but
Torbjørn pointed out that the textile would
be used as upholstery covering for sofas and
chairs, a good reason to slow down on the
colours. We didn't want something too heavy.'

From their studio in Oslo, Anderssen
continues the explanation: 'In our experience,
we've found it easier to concentrate on
texture in the case of furniture. Patterns
can be too invasive. Drop is a nice balance:
it has the high level of expression and
richness that you'd normally expect from
a pattern, paired with the usability of a
textured surface. From a distance, it has a
shimmering monochrome appearance.

When you get closer, though, you can
see the dual colour tones.'

Drop was released in September,
which means we'll have to wait another few
months to discover how it looks on chairs or
sofas. Merckx is as eager as the rest of us to
see this particular application. What she can
tell us for sure is how happy she is about the
ease of the creative process. 'It's a pleasure
to work with young designers. Torbjørn and
Espen have a good feel for colour, textile and
yarns.' Whether the project will ripple into
future collaborations with Anderssen & Voll
remains to be seen, yet one thing's for sure:
Drop is bound to make a few waves. ✕
febrik.com

From Fat

Federico Floriani and Fernando Laposse collected fryer grease from fish-and-chip shops and fat trimmings from butcheries for the project.

Federico Floriani and Fernando Laposse transform animal-fat trimmings into sultry soap sculptures.

WORDS *Adrian Madlener*

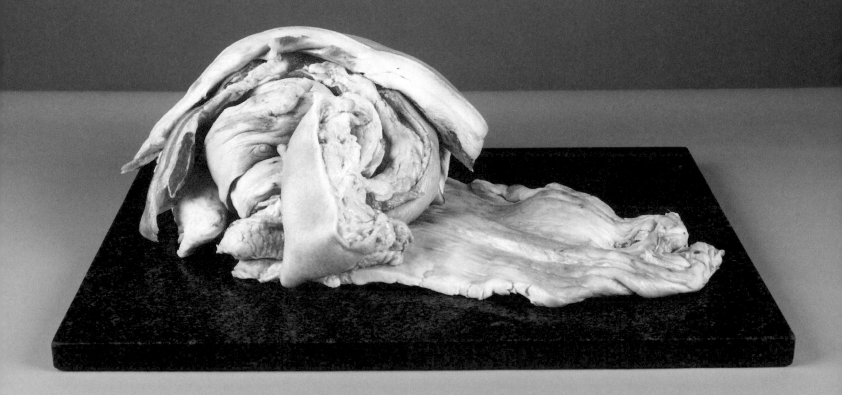

to Artefact

'**WORKING** with the dirtiest stuff out there, we turned fryer grease into beautifully scented textured sculptures,' says Federico Floriani. Partnering with Mexican materials expert Fernando Laposse, Floriani spent two intensive weeks applying lye to upcycle fat to make soap. The irony of *using* fat to *wash* fat was not missed. But the fun didn't stop there: rather than sticking to the standard bar of soap, they opted for a more sophisticated approach. 'Like ceramics, the material is easy to spin or mould and needs no special tools – not even an oven to harden.' The goal, says Floriani, was to create 'beautiful objects' of desire. To achieve this, the duo developed custom utensils to give the saponified fish and beef trimmings a new life and a fresh aesthetic.

Inspired by an old African tradition, the designers fashioned a hair vase and gave it a charcoal-infused, marble-like finish. Followers of the folkloric practice dip horsetail hair into black soap to protect their households from bad spirits. 'We wanted to reinterpret and reinvent the craft by making a vessel with a magic aura and an intriguing narrative.' Such an idea could come only from their shared affinity for the esoteric. Evidently, soap is an unusual material, full of particularities and potential. ✕

fernadolaposse.com
cargocollective.com/federicofloriani

Though not
a fan of plastic,
Christian
Elving – CEO
of Karakter
Copenhagen
– is reissuing
designs by
Joe Colombo,
a man who
owed his fame
to the material.

WORDS *Floor Kuitert*
ILLUSTRATION *Andrea Wan*

Back to Square One

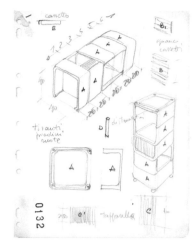

Early sketches show the flexibility of Colombo's Square System. The stackable modules can be combined in countless ways.

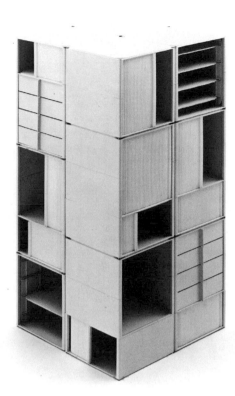

‘In my opinion, plastic doesn't age well’

Joe Colombo
1930-1971

Trained as a painter at the Brera Academy of Fine Arts before studying to be an architect at the Polytechnic University in Milan, Cesare 'Joe' Colombo began his career as a sculptor and painter. He was a member of the 'nuclear art' movement and cofounder of the avant-garde Art Concret Group. In 1959, after taking over the family business in electrical appliances, Colombo began experimenting with new production methods and materials, including plastics. Prior to his untimely death at the age of 41, he headed his own studio in Milan, promoting democratic and functional design through a variety of creative disciplines.

Living Systems

‘Habits change; the interior of rooms has to change with them’: a statement by Joe Colombo that helps to explain his designs. He made flexible, convertible furniture that could adapt to diverse spatial environments and was intended to benefit the user.

‘**J O E** Colombo was the type of designer who could organize a space. He questioned how to create a livable apartment with the use of a well-thought-out furniture arrangement. He believed in democratic, functional design. This is something we promote as well.’ Explaining his decision to reissue Colombo's Square System, originally manufactured by Elco in 1969, is Christian Elving, CEO of Karakter Copenhagen.

Working closely with Studio Joe Colombo, guardian of the Italian designer's legacy, Karakter Copenhagen gave Colombo's stackable multifaceted modules a new lease of life. ‘They had just one example of the design in their archive,’ says Elving. ‘It consisted of two parts that didn't fit together properly. They must have come from different prototypes. We found additional pieces at auctions, but most of the rest is lost.’ Fortunately, Colombo's former assistant Ignazia Favata is now running the studio. ‘She knows a lot about the ideas that went into the design. She's the one who reminded us that “he wouldn't have done it like this”.’

It is not the first Colombo design to be reintroduced by the Danish brand. Il Kilometre, a multipurpose shelving system inspired by a trip to Scandinavia, was on show at last year's Salone del Mobile (*Frame* 105, p. 032).

Karakter Copenhagen maintained the original dimensions of the Square System but chose to execute the design in a different material. Even though Colombo is best known for objects made of plastic – such as the first injection-moulded chair, which he developed with Italian company Kartell – the material didn't suit Karakter's plans. ‘In my opinion, plastic doesn't age well,’ says Elving. But he had another reason to opt for aluminium. ‘We saw a lot of potential in the contract market for the Square System – but only if the modular pieces were sturdier.’ Studio Joe Colombo agreed with him. ‘They understand that companies need to work with materials that meet today's demands.’ ✕

karakter-copenhagen.com
joecolombo.it

The Square System is multifunctional. Modules are suitable as minibars, sideboards, and tables for use in offices, bedrooms, bathrooms and kitchens.

To the Rescue

Beating the traffic by flying above it, Alec Momont's Ambulance Drone could save hundreds of thousands of lives a year.

WORDS *Tracey Ingram* **PHOTO** *Samy Andary*

12

is the number of prototypes Alec Momont developed during the creation of Ambulance Drone

100

kilometres per hour is the speed of the first prototype. Later iterations fly much faster

70

per cent is the survival rate if defibrillation is delivered to patients with ventricular fibrillation within four minutes. Survival rates based on standard methods of emergency response are 8 per cent

1

minute is the average flight time for the first prototype to reach an emergency within a 12-km² zone

4

kilograms is the drone's total weight

800,000

people in the European Union die from cardiac arrest each year

Alec Momont's Ambulance Drone won the Frame Public Award, a prize that was announced at Dutch Design Week 2015. Under Momont's supervision, a team in the Dutch city of Delft has assumed responsibility for further development of the project.
alecmomont.com